2·28·80

This important and original study addresses the religious experience of mankind from the point where James and Whitehead left off. Dr Comfort defines religion as among the consequences of the compelling human experience of an objective "I" (homuncular identity), which engages in a dialogue with the not-I ("That").

Beginning with a highly innovative systems-theory model of the way that "I-ness" is expressed in the nervous system, the book discusses the contribution of oceanic and mystical states to the genesis of world views, the relevance of Hinduism and other systems that have cultivated them, and the way in which religious cosmologies have depicted not "where the world came from" but how the growth of individual self-consciousness creates the known world. Chapters deal with the psychoanalytic and psychosexual aspects of religion, the relevance of insights into "I-ness" to physics and psychiatry, and a striking terminal essay on the human attitude toward death and dying.

This landmark study is one of the few authoritative works, by a scholar equally at home in biology, physics, anthropology and Orientalist studies, to address the new climate of knowledge in which our study of the objective presupposes a study of our way of seeing, and in which objectivist science is seen as being itself a "religion" – one against which William Blake was perhaps the first thinker to protest.

Dr Comfort is a physician, biologist and author both of literary works and of the standard treatise on gerontology. *I and That* is the synthesis of his studies in many different fields and is likely to prove a significant step forward in the transformation of modern scientific awareness in physics, biology, philosophy and medicine.

I AND THAT

NOTES ON
THE BIOLOGY OF RELIGION

ALEX COMFORT
M.B., B.Ch., D.Sc.

CROWN PUBLISHERS, Inc.
New York

I and That

First published in the United States of America in 1979 by
Crown Publishers, Inc.
One Park Avenue,
New York,
N.Y. 10016

Library of Congress Cataloging in Publication Data
Comfort, Alexander, 1920–
I and that.
Includes bibliographical references and index.
1. Religion.   2. Experience (Religion)
I. Title.
BL48.C57   1979   200'.1   79-421
ISBN 0-517-53749-4

Printed in the United States of America

CONTENTS

Acknowledgements

My grateful thanks are due to Prof. Agehananda Bharati and to colleagues at the Institute for Higher Studies who discussed the ideas in this book with me, and to Roger Hearn for his sensitive assistance in setting so rambling a subject into logical order.

Alex Comfort

To the gurus
J. B. S. Haldane, F.R.S (1892–1964)
P. C. Mahalanobis, F.R.S. (1893–1972)

yad vai tad. brahmetīdaṁ vāva tadyo'yam bahirdhā
puruṣād ākāśo yo vai sa bahirdhā puruṣād ākāśaḥ.
ayaṁ vāva sa yo'yam antaḥ puruṣa ākāśo yo vai so'ntaḥ
puruṣa ākāśaḥ

What we call Brahman is extrapersonal space,
the space external to personhood
But that too is what the space within a person is,
in other words intrapersonal space.

Chāndogya Upaniṣad III, 12, 7–8

Foreword

Religion, like lunacy, is a behavior more easily recognized than defined. The emphasis of definition has so far fallen not on the human experience of being, but on the human experience of "the numinous," the recognition of a "supernatural" order of some kind, and on one or both of these as a source of ethical imperatives. This, I think, is a biased presentation: in part it reflects our own cultural uses of religion, and to an even greater extent the actual "religion" of our culture—the deification of the logical–historical mode of perception as against the analogic.

To a biologist, however, religions and religion as normally defined involve a series of homologous or analogous behaviors. He is tempted to look for a structural and adaptive basis for these. He will also note that in our present world there are a number of homologous or analogous activities which seem to have similar functions but do not fit the going definitions. For a start we are not areligious because we have ceased to give great credence to disembodied intelligences, or to rely on them for ethical guidance: we have a number of religion-like behaviors devoid of theology expressed in, say, the "human potential" movement; objective belief in extrapersonal persons persist chiefly at the folkloristic level of "belief," e.g. in ghosts, with the proviso that these are not so much "numinous" or spiritual as imperfectly understood natural phenomena. Meanwhile many social behaviors cognate with theic religions have moved over, complete with the apparatus of response which has gone with them, into psychiatry and nonreligious cults. At the same time we observe behaviors which in other cultures are associated with "religious" practice—ranging from dancing and drumming to charismatic "peak experience" cults, and from hallucinogen consumption to sexual *koinonia*. These are practiced without ritual and at a level of triviality which identifies their aim as novelty or excitement ("kicks," as we say), and yet, if one watches closely, the effects of this apparent trivialization of archaic techniques are often indistinguishable from that of their structured use in a spirit of traditional edification: that is to say, they work *per se*, and sometimes to the alarm of those who engage in them. In other words, there are anthropological resources normally subserving the purposes of structured religion within an ideology which resemble specific drugs in producing specific mental effects, whatever the seriousness or frivolity of our intention in taking them.

I was attracted to this topic by the consideration, born in part of living among the empirical experience-seekers of California, that "religion," being a human behavior, has a biology. In this biology the

11

common factor, so far as I could identify it, between all the behaviors which we recognize as religious, and all those social uses of similar behaviors which we call secular or for-kicks, is that they arise from, and are concerned with manipulating, one much neglected but central human experience, the *homuncular vision* or discursive awareness of "I" as an inner person, separate from "my body," and *a fortiori* from the extra-body environment: the "dwarf sitting in the middle," in the words of the *Katha Upanishad*.

In crude terms, "homuncular identity" means the conviction or experience that there is "someone inside," distinct from the outer world, the body and the brain, in whom the processes of experiencing, willing and so on are focused, and this "someone" objectivizes both these processes and itself. If we look closer, however, this experience does not refer to any soul, true self, inner reality, divine spark, or, indeed, anything so complex as these: such experiences and hypotheses refer to other matters. The inner "someone" who is objectivized in human thinking is a reference point or point of observation on which inner and outer experience are felt to converge, and from which initiatives are felt to issue—not a ghost, but a kind of bottleneck in the circuitry. Rather than representing some transcendental core or hot-spot of being, this self is a point of view, an intrapolated locus round which experience is structured, and like other reference points it is dimensionless and virtual. The fact that we feel it to be there, and arrange experience round it, might well be a simple reflection of our normal sense of position, which carries over into spatial experiences, so that it requires an effort of abstraction to deal with non-three-dimensional space; the result is counterintuitive and requires mathematics to represent it when we succeed. What is neglected and requires explanation is the absolute primacy of this objectivized "standpoint" in human experience, especially in this culture, and the oddity in system theory terms of a perceiving system which acts like this.

Philosophy is, of course, full of discussions of what we mean by, and how we experience, reality; psychiatry is replete with discourses on identity, but there is a quite extraordinary *Vorbeigehen* throughout most of these when it comes to the manner in which self-experience and ontology are point-focused in this surprising manner: most psychiatric discussion of identity turns on what is experienced, how it is interpreted, and how that interpretation is modified, the point focus being taken for granted. Ontology likewise takes the inner reference point as given—we cogitate because it is. The peculiarity of the obvious is not always seen, which is why occasional experiences in which the point of reference and the objectivization of "I" are suppressed are experienced as revelatory—they indicate that a mode of perception which has been taken for granted is conditional: anxiously ruminating schizophrenics who are bothered by such questions as "what is realness?" are experientially closer to the point because their experience is idiosyncratic. Classical psychiatric models have a way, when they deal with "self" or identity, of approaching the issue of homuncular perception and then veering off—Janet's idea of psychasthenia as "loss of the functions of the real," Freud's model of individuation through the recognition of a reality principle, Jung's recognition that parts of inner experience can be objectivized as selves which are not "the" self, Schilder's description of perception as "construction," Klein's observation that babies isolate and incorporate perceived parts of the mother and pattern their learning on that, and Piaget's account of the growth of environmental awareness, all at some point move in the direction of commenting on this reference-point phenomenon and end by assuming it. Freud and Schilder come closest to a confrontation: Freud's model requires that while the recognition of a reality principle individuates, it takes individuation to isolate the "real," and this contains both the development of the homuncular viewpoint and the perception that the inner and the outer world external to the I contain processes beyond volitional control. In Schilder's view, perception does indeed involve construction, but with the wider implication that while the not-I contains arrays, structures are the way-of-seeing of the homuncular viewpoint. The homuncular view-point is normal in that it is "built in."

In addressing "self" the psychiatrist is not basically bothered about the analysis of how humans almost universally perceive, any more than the physician is concerned that they all possess navels or fingerprints—these are in the nature of the beast—and his approach to the exceptions is normative: homuncular I-ness can be upset by drugs, physiological maneuvers and disease states, but it is "normal" if anything is. One reason for this avoidance of the analysis of the homuncular mode is that, in Rollo May's perceptive phrase, anxiety is the state aroused by a threat to "being"—physical death, change in habitual state, or danger to the retention of the homuncular sensation of I-ness, with which more than anything "being" is identified by humans, and the last of these, embodied in human attitudes toward death and in the panic of early schizophrenia, is possibly the most potent. In fact, the homuncular perception of self as not-That and the categorical, or "normal," perception of That are fairly easily dissolved by intensive introspection of the process, and the result of even a slight blurring in this area is often an intense sense of threat, going beyond the philosophical ambiguities which come from viewing "objective reality" as a conditional concept and "self" as a virtual or illusory experience. By contrast "religion" tends to start from the experience of a few individuals in whom I-ness for idiopathic reasons has "slipped," and who are astounded by the insight into perception which springs from the contrast of a nonpositional, observerless, experience; it proceeds through their exhortation to others to "try it and see," and has in some traditions developed nonhomuncular perception as a source of enlightenment and of a true vision of, or oneness with, "That." This may well include all manner of incorporative needs, and almost certainly involves the recreation of early experiences, with all that that entails psychoanalytically, so that initial anxiety is replaced by feelings of bliss, comprehension, universal truth and so on: the model of coming to terms with mystical dissolution of the homuncular view is a little like jumping, with persuasion, into cold water and finding it exhilarating once the initial shock is over. A harder-nosed view, however, finds its real rewards in the fact that an alternative mode of structuring the I–That relationship throws a flood of light on the whole process of "objective" observation—the religion of our own culture—and reveals a great deal about its structure. Indeed, although a few psychiatrists and philosophers have dabbled in the examination of "mysticism" in all periods, and some, rather than jumping, have been thrown in by peculiarities of their cerebral organization, the modern revival of interest in the painstaking attempts of yogis and others to create nonhomuncular states of mind by elaborate inner manipulation comes from the rediscovery of a far more primitive mode of access at a much cheaper rate—the chemical substances acting on the median rhaphe which alter or suppress the homuncular viewpoint. This is of course not the first time that "religion" has patterned "psychiatry" or "philosophy," but it is the first time since the advent of the scientific revolution that it has done so by the creation of empirical experiences which comment on the validity of normal objectivism. It is for that reason that I have aimed this book at the biology of religion rather than that of philosophy.

Formal philosophy would have been a less useful paradigm. The homuncular idiosyncracy, if one can call it that, has been its Godot—the constantly present *dramatis persona* who never in fact appears. Kant, by a prodigious effort, manages to drag it into the wings but never quite on-stage. What strikes us now in reading his remarks on the paralogisms of transcendental psychology is not only how much he contributed to the elbow-room of mathematical physics by recognizing time and space as structures, but how enormously the universe of discourse has changed. The change has been in the direction of reinstating what our ancestors called natural philosophy: its components have been the immense success of scientific objectivism and the extension of this, as a simple necessity of the process of getting on with science, to the mental apparatus involved in "doing science" at all. We have to make sense of homuncular vision and its effects on empirical observation in order to get on with empirical observation. The point which strikes us today about formal philosophy is not that it asked the wrong questions—it asked nearly all the right ones at different times and under different guises—but simply that if we take a different paradigm, the practical comprehension of observations in physics and the practical comprehension of observations in neurology, "how" questions rather than "why" questions, we are forced to develop empirical techniques of treating the material, and when we do so the Maginot Lines erected by the immense cerebral efforts of one philosophical period and then frontally assaulted by the next are found to have been simply outflanked. Tolerance of ambiguity, routine use of laws and hypotheses as approximations, and a total disinterest in absolutes except as pitons to which climbing-ropes can be attached are now standard intellectual equipment not for "doing philosophy" but for "doing science" with such purely practical aims as building a fusion reactor or treating dementias. One could perfectly well, given modern information, go back to Kant, or Plato, or Hume's discussion of causality, and tackle the issues of homuncularity and knowledge from there—but quite apart from the unfairness of this in using up thesis material which could graduate large numbers of indigent scholars in the nonplaying disciplines, it is simply not the style of the times: and it is precisely the change of style brought about by objective and experimental science which makes it possible to say anything new in this area.

The formulation of the epistemological importance of I-ness has in fact been left to physics, in which techniques for developing a counterintuitive model of "reality" have made it unavoidable—physicists such as Mach and Heisenberg make no bones about the contingency of objective phenomena. Our normal, and for ordinary purposes necessary, perception of the objective, of causality, and of such things as linear time is perfectly adequate over the range of data-processing in which it presumably evolved, rather as for ordinary purposes the ground is best taken to be flat—with further extrapolation, however,

> "the conception of objective reality has evaporated . . . into a mathematics that represents no longer the behavior of elementary particles, but rather our knowledge of this behavior . . ."[1]

or more correctly our peculiar mode of perceiving it, in that "nature" consists of arrays, while we perceive it in terms of structures:

> "there is no cause or effect in nature: nature simply *is*: recurrence of like cases . . . exists but in the abstraction which we perform for the purpose of mentally reproducing facts . . ."[2]

The magnitude of the revolution brought about by focusing attention on the conditionality of the homuncular experience has not yet been fully appreciated, as we have seen. In fact, it generates a neorationalism with the following postulates:

1. That "nature" consists of arrays, on which human mentation imposes structure
2. That phenomena, which are our only contact with these arrays, are exactly what their name implies, namely "appearings" in which structure has been so imposed
3. That in some instances what appear to be phenomena—time is an example—may turn out to be wholly structures: wholly consequences, that is, of a particular manner of intuitivist data-processing.

What was a subjective intuition of "mysticism" now appears as a necessary postulate derived from our culture's own source of sacramental knowledge, the observation of objective reality by controlled experimentation.

This bears some resemblance to Plato's cave-and-shadow model but is a great deal harder-nosed, in that whatever is casting the shadows, the "ideal forms" exist in a tangible place, the pattern-store of the human sensorium. Accordingly it becomes intensely interesting, not merely from the standpoint of neurology or curiosity, but from the practical angle of interpreting exactly what we mean by the objective, to examine what the world would look or feel like if it were experienced with the sense of homuncular viewpoint suppressed. The immense energy spent by humans in many traditions in recreating this experience as "enlightening" does now seem retrospectively justified in terms of our own prosaic valuation of enlightenment, and not merely because it produces euphoria or awe at the novelty of the sensation.

I began to make these notes in the first instance in response to a colleague who was threatening to make a study of the "influence of religion in contemporary America" without, it seemed to me, any clear idea of the scope of the behaviors he intended to include as religious. It would be pointless to argue about this, since every investigator has the right to mark out an area with his own definitions, and the conventional or the anthropological definitions of "religious behavior" could serve in this case. The advantage of treating "religion" as a behavior arising from the peculiarity of human identity—what a man does with his I-ness—is that, aside from opening up a more precise attempt to put I-ness into intelligible terms of systems theory, it very greatly widens the formative scope upon ideas and behavior of "religion" beyond anything which conventional dogmas or religious ideologies could now attain by way of influence—indeed the time has long passed when the Catholic or Hindu physicist was much bothered in his physics by his Catholicism or his Hinduism; though Hinduism, being relatively nondogmatic, or having the potential of being so, can actually provide insights relevant to physics. The comprehension of I-ness, our unspoken assumptions about it, and even our view of where it ends and the environment begins, are of practical and not merely philosophical relevance to any sensible attempt either to extract "meaning" from observations or to gain an epistemology of science.

The non-Democritean universe has been with us for a full half-century, and most scientists are vaguely familiar with its outlines. The striking fact is that in spite of the revolutionary intellectual implications, neither the limited high priesthood which actually works in particle physics, nor the vast mass of lay believers, finds that the revolution affects conventional or middle-order perceptions at all. This is because the ontology of physics is probably the first philosophical model of an innovative kind which bears no relation to conventional experience and which cannot be empathically visualized—not only is it difficult, but visualization would contravene what appear to be invincible modes of conventional experience. This is the real importance of neurological studies, and of examining unconventional modes of experience. The justification for concentrating on those which appear to bypass homuncularity is not the pursuit of some kind of nonrational source of knowledge, but the fact that while science, starting from naive objectivism, has been able by the force of experiment and mathematical analysis to develop a counterintuitive model of perception empirically, one sizeable human tradition arrived at the same counterintuitive model without any physical experimentation by cultivating mental states in which it was not inferred but actually experienced. It seems perfectly rational therefore to ask whether the direct experience might not greatly increase our capacity for further inference, in retrospect if not while it was actually going on. More important, it might actually lead to the incorporation of the new model of ontology into ordinary experience by making it felt as well as inferred. Other speculative models up to the time of Einstein (and even including some very abstract creations, such as those of the Gnostics and the neo-Platonists) actually affected the way that their adherents lived and their attitudes toward unbiddable portions of real-time experience such as death. Oriental philosophies which cultivated nonhomuncular experiences did so precisely because they do reorder experience, not in the direction of refusing to sit on a chair because it is not a solid object, or of refusing to avoid a mad elephant because it too is Brahman, but in the direction of a world perception and self-perception which was devoid of violent jolts and gear changes, and in which a good many standing human anxieties and obsessions (death and immortality are the leading example) were strikingly reordered. There is something odd about a society which is able to infer relativistic time for one set of entirely practical objectives, and which continues to live in terms of flat-earth, literalistic and nineteenth-century objectivism as its religious or style-setting mode. Physicists, even the most rarefied of them, might not be too bothered by this discrepancy, but for a social psychiatrist interested in the development of cultural styles it suggests the imminence of a major transition.

The fact of the matter is that when we talk about "I" we are combining two things—an experience and a hypothesis. The experience is so universal as to be a convention which we do not address: in fact, in addressing almost anything by way of language we have to adopt it. The hypothesis is the resulting formalism: a hypothesis in Medawar's sense of a crystallizing intuition with testable implications, not a Euclidean proposition.

It will be evident that there is a very close analogy between the intuitive use we make of "I" and the intuitive use we make of time-as-linear-sequence. Time is a Kantian *a priori*, not a thing: it is the way in which we experience rather than an experience of a thing. On the other hand time is measurable and directional, at least in middle-range phenomena, and its contingency can be got at mathematically, as in Einsteinian space-time. "I" is both more *a priori* still and far messier to dissect, because in any process of intellection an "I" is doing the cogitating, and a loop is built in from the start, in mathematics, in language, and even into the intuitive sense of having got a plausible answer.

The "scientific" way of getting round this (again in Medawar's rubric for the scientific, not the popular model) is to imagine if we can what physics, mathematics, cognition, or the scenery would look like if seen by a being which did not refer them to a positional "I"—or rather, because I-ness is a modifier of experience as much as of formalisms to describe experience, what these things would feel like in an I-less mode—the equivalent of a non-Euclidean geometry of Suchness. This is precisely what oceanic "mystics" do, or have done—they have hit upon a device, dodge, state, or pathological condition (possibly several or all of these) in which perception is experienced as I-less: not, of course, or not initially as the contrived variation of experience which we would call an experiment, but quite certainly in the first place by sheer accident. The result, however, is an observation, not a fantasy—it fits the Baconian exclusionary rules in being consistent, having a structure which crosses all manner of cultural and preconceptual boundaries, and sounding exactly the same in report whether the observer was a yogi, a Christian monk, a Zen novice, a Hopi Indian or an Eskimo. The first three of these might possibly have common cultural preconceptions—hardly the last two. Each adds a totally different cultural superstructure but is fairly clearly describing the same sensation.

Where this experience differs from others, however, is that it affects the felt world as well as the rationalized or described world: it goes to the roots of intellection, by providing a wholly unconventional contrast to ordinary or logical ways of seeing. That, if we think about it a moment, is really unique. It represents the difference between creating intellectually, say, a Riemannian geometry, perceiving by mathematical analysis of observations that "space is curved," and actually seeing curved space as an intuitively visualizable model on all fours with conventional, domestic space. Most people find space-time models difficult precisely because they cannot be intuited conventionally. Non-I-dependent perception is even harder to envisage by an imaginative effort: which is why the experience, when it does occur, is so uniquely impressive.

The bearing of this on the biology of religion is not that some mystics are vociferously religious—some oceanic states are entirely secular and occur in the vociferously irreligious—but rather that it already, on quite other grounds, makes semantic sense to see "religious" behaviors as containing as their core various I-delimiting concerns, however much else they also contain.

If science as we normally understand it is the attempt to draw objective conclusions from observations, it is an I-delimiting experience or activity—one moreover conducted by persons who are "I"s and must pass all of their observational input and interpretative output through the circuitry involved in the human identity experience. Even computers bear the mark of Adam because his descendants programmed and targeted them.

If "religion" involves the manipulation of our experience of I in relation to our experience of not-I (environment, other persons, Nature, the gods, "reality," or in the Hindu terminology simply "That") then the religious ideology of our own culture is linear objectivism: we regard the environment, including the neurology on which our experiences depend, as "real", and the temporal progression which we observe in it as real-time, and we deify or numinize the observer, who "is" by virtue of cogitating. This looks uncommonly like a systems break in our intellectual armor which has arisen simply through neglect to look at the implications of our notion—which is basically a subjective intuition—of identity: our militant objectivity has a subjectivity at its intellectual heart. Accordingly, to pursue this idea as far as it will go and discuss "religious" behaviors in this light, it is necessary first of all to spend some time on this remarkable experience.

Notes on Sanskrit words

As the language of philosophy is Greek or German, so the language of empirical religio–neurologic experience is Sanskrit. In writing a book of this kind one is forced to raid Sanskrit for terminology, not as a branch of higher lifemanship but for lack of precise equivalents.

It would be possible to translate on every occasion that such a borrowing is made. However, in the interests of brevity, the following Sanskrit idea-words can be listed in advance.

advaita	"not-double"—state of mind in which all, including the self, is perceived as one and without distinction.
bhaktī	"devotion"—religious attitude analogous to sexual infatuation, charismatic devotionalism, *Schwärmerei*.
ćakra	"circle"—hypothetical point in body image on which yogi focuses attention. Points are envisaged as being situated along the spine from perineum to top of head.
ćakra-pūja	"circle worship"—ritual group sex, usually with randomly selected partners, as culmination of the Five Sacraments of Tantrik left-hand worship (the others are meat, fish, wine, and parched grain).
dvaita	"double"—state of mind in which two entities only, "I" and "all else," are perceived, all other distinctions being collapsed into one-ness. Stage preceding and inferior to *advaita* perception, which abolishes this last distinction.
līlā	"play"—the sport of the gods in the creation and destruction of illusory diversity.
māya	"illusion"—process by which the original One is experienced as subdivided into many (objects, experiences, self and environment, etc.). The state of mind antithetic to *advaita vedanta*; the normal state of perception.
murtī	"manifestation"—any expression of a god or an aspect of a god—image, manifestation, form. The persons of the Trinity, an ikon, and a thaumaturgic saint are all *murtīs* of the Christian deity.

nirvīkalpa "non-conceptual"—experience which is immediate and not conceptually analyzed and which creates no categories is *nirvīkalpa*; "right hemisphere" perception.

paśu "tethered domestic beast"—formally and ritually religious person devoid of empirical religious experience.

rās maṇḍala "love circle"—the Vaiṣṇava ritual equivalent to the Śaiva "circle worship"—group sex re-enacting the sport of Kṛṣṇa with the milkmaids.

sādhana "trip, exercise"—any schedule or program undertaken to achieve a spiritual end, whether conventional or idiosyncratic. When Ramakrishna impersonated first Sita the bride of Rama, and then Hanuman, his monkey lieutenant, to achieve a vision of Rama himself, these exercises were *sādhana*. Other *sādhanas* are prayer, yoga, and worldly activity.

sadhu holy man, professional religious empiric.

samādhi "equalization"—the state of suppressed identity-experience which is the universal object of yoga: state in which "I" and "That" are perceived as non-different: oceanic state.

śaktī "spear, power"—female emanation or counterpart of a deity personifying energy and creating diversity by generating *māya*, as against the quality of immanence conceived as male. Female partner of a yogi by coition with whom the original dyad is mystically re-formed.

tapas "heat"; any ordeal or violent manipulation
pl. *tapāsya* undertaken to "light a fire" under consciousness—askesis, work-out, austerity. The "ordeals" of an athlete, a Marine or an astronaut in training are *tapāsya*.

vīra "hero"; Tantrik adept who attempts to obtain full enlightenment by empirical religious experience rather than adherence to orthodoxy; experimental *sadhu*.

I.1
Identity

The human sense of identity—the fact that we experience ourselves as agents, displaying volition, operating "our" body as if it were a machine distinct from the I which operates it, is the most familiar of all human experiences; and perhaps upon inspection, the oddest. We cannot recall the genesis of the I—it became gradually possessed of self-awareness around the age of two or three—and we dislike the idea of its dissolution in death. We have devoted enormous and gratuitous mental energy to finding reasons why the illusion of I-ness as distinct from the material brain should in fact be a reality, and the I immortal, or at least recyclable, at a supernatural level. Oddest of all, since this is a cherished human experience, it seems logically probable that were it possible to construct an electromechanical system of a complexity identical with our brain's bioelectrical system, it too would have a sense of identity and selfhood—if not, there are fairies at the bottom of our garden, or some reservations (which we will discuss later) apply; the machine might have first to go through the experience of human individuation. Animals, though they do not have the acute split, so far as we can judge, between a logical conscious and a repressed "unconscious" mind which has evolved in man (largely, Freud and modern primatology would infer, to avoid some problems arising from progeny–father competition in a long childhood[3]) do appear to possess introspective experience of a complexity varying with their brain structure and social behavior. One is tempted to infer that "consciousness" in some degree, though it is not the same thing as human I-ness, may be a property inherent in all problem-solving systems—an old human intuition which has been extended to include the Universe as a problem-solving "organism" and make that conscious too, in a manner of speaking.

If a pig had a "sense of identity" comparable to that of man, it would presumably experience it from birth. Being precocial, that is to say, born able to walk and forage, birth for such a discursive piglet would have to be an experience closely similar to that which we normally experience in waking. The human experience is clearly different; we are altricial mammals born with much less, or a much more selective, immediate grasp on our environment—chiefly touch, sound and possibly odor, plus taste. Accordingly we "wake" gradually: if there is an incident in which I-ness first becomes concrete, as there may be an incident in which we first discover we can walk, or read, it precedes memory and we do not explicitly recall it. The sense of I-ness is suppressed during anesthesia or fainting and returns sharply with recovery ("Where am I?"). It is not suppressed during sleep accompanied by dreams—waking involves rather a sudden regeneration of real-time I-ness, unless preceding sleep has been very deep, when it involves a sudden reactivation of identity like that of anesthetic recovery. The body-image distortions (getting larger or smaller, like Alice) which some people experience during the onset of sleep (hypnagogic hallucinations) are alarming or unpleasant partly because I-ness is not lost; but a monitoring function close to it, our body-image, with which I-ness maintains a constant dialog, is irrationally changed. This dialog is what Freud means by saying that our ego is "first and foremost a body ego."[4] Some people react with a similar anxiety to a sudden change in the configuration of their teeth felt with the tongue-tip. The point here is that I-ness is closely connected with body image but not identical with it—the illusion of "driver" and "vehicle" is preserved, the body image being the vehicle: in fact, in driving a car we add it to our body image and may even use it to communicate by nonverbal gestures with other drivers.

In fact, the most striking feature of the I-experience once established is its relative invulnerability. It is unaffected by aphasia, agnosia, apraxia, cerebral bisection or massive brain damage short of permanent unconsciousness. Psychedelics can attack it: under LSD people may feel multiple or have the illusion of some kind of mental co-pilot—the sensation schizophrenics commonly verbalize as "being influenced with waves," or they may have *samādhi*-like experiences of the blurring of boundaries: here the I-sense is certainly not functioning as usual—on the other hand, the phrase "they have experiences" implies that it is not suppressed: someone is monitoring something, even if it does not feel like it. Whether catatonia represents I-sense in abeyance I do not know—recovered catatonics report having been far more aware of their surroundings than they appeared to observers to be. The "influence" or "multiple" sensations of LSD, delirium or schizophrenia represent noise-effects in some part of the I-ness process, often with the I trying to fight them off and re-establish normal function. Really bizarre divisions of identity, popular with popular writers, where there are several "identities" who may or may not know one another or have access to one another's experiences are often the result of injudicious psychiatric suggestion and are usually said to be hysteric, though this may only mean that we do not know what causes them. The extreme case of the co-pilot/pilot phenomenon is "possession," an old human religious resource in which the conative or operant part of I-ness, which is concerned with initiating actions, is hijacked, or voluntarily handed over by the everyday I. In the "stationary states" of Parkinsonism I-ness is unimpaired but conation and thought become "stuck."

Accordingly, in even the heaviest trips produced by psychedelic agents or by disease the I-sense is surprisingly invulnerable—it may seem attacked (by unwanted co-pilots) or be referred to the environment (the vehicle is handling abnormally, the scene is altered, the "backdrop" of consciousness modified), but someone is still monitoring. This, of course, may be a circular argument—if the monitoring were to stop, there would be no way for outside observers to debrief the subject afterwards. It is unclear, for example, what happens to I-ness in postepileptic automatism—the recovered subject, being amnesic, may have been experiencing himself or not, even though his actions have been complex. The same goes for post-traumatic amnesias—boxers have gone several rounds and even won a fight without any subsequent recall. Unless we had an electrical or similar way of monitoring I-ness processes this argument is unprofitable.

With regard to major structural failures in the brain, it could be that unconsciousness is simply the nonfunction of identity in both its operant and monitoring aspect. On the other hand, there is a lot of evidence that "vegetable" head-injury cases, and even lightly anesthetized subjects, may be in possession of an intact and functioning I-ness and only unable to communicate, to an extent not guessed by those around them. Other bizarre and well-documented changes in I-sense include so-called astral projection, in which the body image is objectified, the I appears to float above or outside it or to travel in the Spirit leaving the body behind, a condition occurring under the influence of LSD or meditation, in terminal illness, or spontaneously, which has played a part in religious idea-making; and autoscopic hallucination, in which identity remains internal, but the whole body image is projected as a fetch, or external ghostly double.

I.2
Identity and pattern

Art and iconography objectify the "feel" of identity. The classic example here is the mandala, a quadrilaterally symmetrical pattern, square or circular, which is used either as a schema for the "self," or for a real or imaginary cosmos, or for both. As a physiological original it appears to represent the projection of the retinal fields on the visual cortex (or at least *è ben trovato se non è vero*, the two are the same shape). In Hindu and Buddhist art many maṇḍalas are also *yantras*, i.e. diagrams intended to facilitate or induce meditative states of mind—partly through emblematic and symbolic content, which causes the meditator to alternate between the contemplation of the whole and of the parts of the diagram. They may perhaps also operate through a low key equivalent of photic drive arising from the contemplation of colored segments in order. Used schematically in this way the maṇḍala is an example of pattern-generator/pattern-analyzer interaction in the nervous system. As a schema for the "self," the diagram usually has "gates" (inputs)[5] on four sides, and an elaboration of concentric layers. What actually does duty for the "self" in its most refined experience is the center of the diagram, which these onionlike layers surround. This may be occupied by something symbolic (yin/yang, male/female, or another dyad), but psychologically one has the impression that what should occupy the middle of a truly schematic maṇḍala/diagram of I-ness is a vortex or black hole.[6]

Human ingenuity has naturally blown up this series of imaginative and symbolic variations on "what we see with our eyes closed" into innumerable uses, from cosmology to the design of temples, but Jung was right to select it, since it is one of the few such schemata where the neurological basis of the diagram can be inferred, and where it probably represents some kind of zero-input display, intimately connected both with vision in three dimensions and also with our appreciation of symmetry, both intensely associated with the way that "identity" is experienced. In this sense, the maṇḍala is not only a diagram of the experience but arguably an actual part of it; and the drawings made of such by primitives and not-so-primitives are one of the best examples of outputs from the human pattern-mechanism which can be played back into it.

Of Jung's two identity-expressing schemata, the other is the tree (of life, etc.); but this, unlike the maṇḍala which reflects structure and static experience, is rather obviously an emblematic expression of process (trees grow, and eventually produce flowers and fruit) commenting on the changes which the self or the cosmos or both experience, and hence it is in a sense anecdotal. It is instructive, I think, to contrast these two human models conveying information symbolically: the second, though not arbitrary, does not tell us much either about the nervous system or (if we were showing them to a Martian with other experiences of self than ours) about how I-ness feels—the first, the maṇḍala, does.

I.3
The "dwarf in the middle"

The image of the vessel and the pilot is, of course, Aristotle's—and is summarily rejected by Merleau-Ponty on the rather odd ground that, were it correct, we should not speak as we do indeed speak of "my" ship, and treat such a vehicle as a surrogative extension of "my" body. Much tiresome philosophy arises from ignoring the fact that the homuncular I has two sources of input regarding the bodily environment—the general range of perceptions, and the body image, and these are by no means identical. In Aristotle's model they correspond to the visual and the instrument perceptions of the pilot, but the body image, so far from being an instantaneous or immediate readout, incorporates all manner of corrections and biases which may cause it to differ fundamentally from the true state of the body, and the interpretations (for the body image is interpretative or communicative) placed on that state by others, so that a robust person may perceive himself as small, and so on. The perception of smallness may not enter into his personal navigation (when he buys shoes or walks under a branch) but does appear in his body image, leading us to inquire into the significance which such illusory smallness has for him in terms of past experience and, in particular, of interpersonal relations. One component of body image, then, is a projection of how we appear to the sensorium of others. Another (it is not now clear exactly how these two are related) is an element of internal scan, covering not so much the organs as the systems which monitor the organs: this is the area of such mental but consistent structures as the yogic *ćakras* and *suṣumnā*, which are not "organs" anatomically, but descriptions of introspection directed at our own nervous system. Biofeedback research and yogic tradition, apart from modern psychiatric experience, suggest that by manipulating the body image we can manipulate the body. It is also the area from which parts of the self-experience are projected as personages—both in dreams and in theogonies.

I shall have more to say about these projections in talking about the fauna of religious formulations—the persons of such theogonies. My point here is that because of the conventional experience that I am distinct from and an objective observer of my brain, when parts of the self-experience process not central to I-ness are perceived, they must needs be perceived as part of a body image. This has two consequences: one is that there is a kind of body-image environment distinct from non-body inputs which is readily experienced as an analog of a cosmos, and hence as a model of one (we shall come later to Blake's very sophisticated exploration of this twinning of microcosm and macrocosm in mystical poetry); the other is that where such perceived impressions from the peripheral mechanisms involved in identity have a component of self-ness (where, in other words, they are plugged in fairly closely to some part of I but not so closely as to be introjected into it) they more or less must be projected as "other" selves, which, since they are not "our" self are simply others, but others related to the I as the body image is related. Spirits and numina which carry conviction and fit archetypal structures, as well as personalized figures in dreams, are very commonly of this kind. Others, such as heroes, who contain aspirations rather than a portion of introspected self, are chiefly emblematic, less august and less archetypally efficacious. With true projections from the periphery of I, like Jung's Shadow Self or even Blake's Four Zoas, the assimilation is immediate, and it is this immediacy which is typical of "religious" experience. Even the exoticism of Blake's presentation does not prevent the "Divine Family" of his theogony having an impact of acceptance as our family—the "answering chord" effect common to archetypes we cannot discursively explore, from Jesus Christ to the Tarot cards. Most of the religious theogonies in use have, unlike Blake's, been polished as the Tarot cards have been to a fine degree of fit with the human pattern-sending mechanism, which they appear to activate.

Although I-ness is apparently localized "inside" (or just behind) us, so that the letter E traced on the forehead of a blindfolded subject is read "from behind" as the figure 3, a large part of the experience is obviously transactional rather than purely proprioceptive. Quite apart from learning-components in its development, and the dependence of self-image on social interaction (it is arguable how much I-ness a person would have if totally isolated from birth) it is rapidly upset by sensory deprivation, to an extent almost equal to the effects of deliriant drugs, the consequences of which closely resemble those of sensory-deprivation experiments. It is accordingly feedback-dependent, but the feedback element appears to operate by setting the boundaries of the I which is experienced.

Remarkably little modern analytic thought has been devoted to I-ness at a practical rather than a philosophically rarefied level. It merits our attention, however, both because of its immense influence in determining the set of our philosophical and scientific formulations (which would be totally different if we experienced ourselves differently) as well as of ideas such as liberty or individualism, and because, unless we are *enragé* psychovitalists, it ought to be accessible to systems and simulation research—the main problem here being to determine when it is present.

A friend of mine is deeply involved in research upon cloning—

he wishes to immortalize himself in an unlimited edition. It is impossible to convince him that though innumerable Frankenstein-men could thinkably be programmed to behave like John Doe, and even share John Doe's experience, there is no way of plugging in the original John Doe's identity-sense to their continuing and ongoing experience, any more than to that of conventional grandchildren. Such is our unawareness of an experience which enters radically into every abstract or concrete idea we express, and every action "we" initiate. How do "we" initiate actions, anyway? And what exactly (under the conventional name of "freewill") sets such actions in train?

Close introspection of the I-experience is one way of inducing alarming yogic dissociation and a possible reason for our neglect to examine so general an experience may lie in the threat which insight would pose to the universal conventions underlying human thought and action. With the growth of neurology, neuropharmacology and computer science it is bound to come, however. It will be interesting to see what the analysis of I-ness does to the I in the cultural term—probably little, in view of its convenience, as the discovery that the Earth is round affected mariners but not pedestrians, and mariners only at one remove from "commonsense" perception. Provided, that is, that our insight into what I-ness is does not widen still further our capacity to tamper with it.

I.4
Logicality, linearity, and Gestalt perception

One possible consequence of the homuncular way in which we experience ourselves is connected with the rather sharp split which exists in man between linear and analog modes of thinking—so sharp, in fact, that Ornstein[7] locates them in opposite cerebral hemispheres (if he is right, the invention of handed literacy may well have produced striking differences in conceptualization between the literate and the verbal cultures). Whether this division into what look like compartments is a result of our odd psychosexual development, which reverses direction, as it were, and requires a block-out of some early learning, or whether it facilitated the evolution of that pattern, it does at first sight look as if the experience of the homunculus as an objective viewer thinking thoughts but having little direct access to much of the analog or "unconscious" matter is a reflection of the objectivism we normally feel.

Much "humanistic" psychology is based on giving value or importance to the analogic and imaginative. Both psychiatric and religious manipulations often aim to extend the homunculus' field of vision—basically on the ground that beside self-consciousness the homunculus has "felt" experiences such as affect which modify its set, or alter the way in which I-ness is experienced and facts are ordered or interpreted. The I-experience can be treated behavioristically as the sum of learned reactions to total body and environmental experience, but the way in which it is objectified looks as if it may be evolved and neurologically built it. Yet even here there seems to be a wide choice of which circuitry will be called into play. I-modifying experiences, whether behavioral like religio-psychologic mind-blowing or pharmacological as with LSD, can permanently alter the backdrop of the I-experience beyond that general in the culture—basically by exposing the I to a new experience or placing it in a new viewpoint. The new information, however, comes from inside the nervous system, and much of it belongs to the reordering of the body image which the I is perceived as scanning. These manipulations are, for us, socially artificial: whether they were accidentally discovered by primitive man as psychedelic mushrooms were accidentally discovered, and whether the possibility of using them is adaptive, we can only speculate. The strictly linear I has been highly adaptive in producing intentionality and science, and is only disadaptive in its capacity for ignoring other equally active motives beside linearity which can play hell with our illusionary self-image of purpose. It also represents one-half only of our resources of conceptualization.

One part of the ideology of the all-objective homunculus (which gets to look more of a culture-artefact the longer we consider it—the Responsible Democratic Protestant I) is the body of logic and philosophy—these are rationalizations for being linear-minded. "Thinking" in a Cartesian sense is one of the things that the homunculus "does"—as it "decides" to buy stock or order the big toe to move. It also "sees" pattern and "establishes" natural laws or "makes" discoveries. These are more culturally-biased experiences which we take for granted as we do the "we" which engages in toe-moving, but they are odd in the extreme. We cannot "see the seer of seeing, or think the thinker of thinking."[8] Four things are somehow getting articulated—the I experience, the body image (which is part of the I's observing equipment), cultural training, and something called the environment, which includes everything except the hypothetical I—an odd assortment, all fuzzy and all interacting (the actual body, on which all these operations including I-ness depend, is treated as part of the environment—circularity can go no further).

A clearer picture can be got from forgetting the thinking I for a while—the black box, the nervous system, is both pattern generator and pattern analyzer, and the patterns it generates and those it "sees" depend on the same circuitry. A few patterns, like wave-motion as a principle, depend on synesthetic intuition followed by analysis (the bringing to the notice of I of the structure of an intuition). Others are generated, probably, by the fortuitous fit between pieces of body-image perception and things going on outside. Science—and ideological linearity—consist in checking out to exclude those which are wholly arbitrary; they constitute many "archetypes" and a large part of the mythopoetic machine—the chief feature of which is that whatever one puts in by way of input comes out made over into an archetypal form, whether the question asked be a factual one like the origins of the solar system or a random assemblage. The effect of going through this shaping is to make the output, whatever its content, carry a disabling sense of intuitive "fit," unsurprising when we consider how it was arrived at—of course, it "fits," as a waffle fits a waffle-iron. The interest of this for our view of the self is that it is the I which is convinced, or even converted, by such inputs, and which experiences the feeling of "rightness" in them.

Originally, what "we" perceive of the "environment" is most likely adaptive—we perceive what and how best enables us to survive under the conditions in which man evolved. But with the development of a social and imaginative I the whole thing has become more complex; the pattern-generating and pattern-analyzing system involve echoes off parts of our nervous program which make up all the psychoanalytic fauna of subsidiary selves experienced by the usual I as alien or not-self (anima, shadow-self, deities, introjected parents, culture symbols). We have also—and partly because of the disturbing effect, on us, of any sensed ambiguity or multiplicity—a very active search for external I-manageable pattern which makes us extremely uneasy if we cannot create one or harmonize those we create.

To put this discursively (for this I to expose it to other I's) is difficult; it can however be very simply done in the sinistral, or analogic, mode by way of poetry—Wallace Stevens's poem "The Idea of Order at Key West" is an attempt of this kind (we hear order in sea-music which suggests a coherent voice but is contentless; is this order (a) in the periodicities of the water, (b) in our heads, (c) in the fact that where there is pattern, even though complex, our "rage for order" abstracts?) It is actually an interesting comment on the types of economy and of redundancy in our brain, which, because we are social animals, is angled to inter-I communication, that this kind of matter can be most economically "sent" in a highly allusive poem. A poem, like a myth, is a very efficient patterned input to the maximum number of these engrammatic models, with low specificity (high redundancy) but high economy. Written out in plain for the I-logical system to read, it would be prohibitively long, like a detailed gloss on *Finnegan's Wake*, but more specific.

I have digressed on logicality and the two modes because, although they do not bear wholly on, or coincide with, the experience I set out to look at, namely homuncular vision, the philosopher in Western thought has himself been traditionally a rather hubristic blowup of the homunculus, not only toe-moving but idea-moving, and being because he cogitates. The blast of intuitivism, mythologism and general antirationalism which is now blowing is not really exempt from the philosophical tradition—it simply substitutes irrational structures for pseudorational ones. What needs to be done, at the present time, is that we remove our viewpoint from both; "logical" formulations represent one mode of the brain; "analogic," another—both useful for different purposes, but liable to spill illicitly the one into the other. Linear science is probably the "best" way of, say, inferring and verifying the existence of black holes. Analogic myth is a good way of scanning the interaction of social needs, body image, and our posse of "selves," of which the I is only the sheriff.

One senses an uncertainty-principle bar to using the I to produce an *empathic* or experienced analysis of I-ness, and the result of success in doing so might be a samādhi-like dissolution of that necessary experience alarming to the unprepared. Descartes put his evidence of the reality of personal existence in three words, each one of which we would now question. If I think that the livable answer to the questions raised by our recognition of the conditionality of sovereign reason is likely to come from looking at the biology of mind and of self-experience, that may be occupational prejudice, but it has some hard evidence on its side.

The quality of human I-ness may look uniform to us, but this may be the result of prejudice: both it, and the valuation (rather than the minute-by-minute perception) of time must be culturally set, at least to some extent. The Australian Aborigine contrasts "present" not with "past" and/or "future" but with "sacred" (dream-time, *tjukurpa*)[9] and equates linguistically father's father with children's children. He has thus two cells of classification, I = now, and That. This shows a striking insight, unparalleled in our philosophical language, into I-ness as being also now-ness: "then" and "future" belong in the realm of That, for they are only indirectly accessible to the I by extrapolation.

I.5
Some constraints on linearity

Not least of the conditions upon linear thinking is the existence of pattern ingrained in the machinery with which we perceive pattern. Most people are aware that it is difficult to write absolute nonsense, however much the record of academic philosophy might suggest otherwise, because in free-associating arbitrary or nonsensical matter we are using a nonrandom mechanism. The structures discovered with such excitement by William Yeats in occultism and in his wife's trances, the matter of folklore and myth, the "group unconscious" of Jung, and the esoterica now in revival which so excite the nonlinear-minded are not arbitrary and vain imaginings. Misleading they undoubtedly are if we take them literally. What they represent is the playback, not of external pattern, but of the structure of our pattern-selecting mechanism.

How this mechanism is situated in respect to the wiring of the I experience is at present anybody's guess. We have a "group unconscious," not in the sense of an intraspecific form of ESP, but as all IBM computers of the same model have a "group unconscious," some aspects of which reflect software, some hardware wiring, and yet others the geometry of hole-spacing in punch cards; in other words it is structural, and it is the structure through and with which the homuncular I looks out, and the structure it sees as zero-input display when it attempts to look in.

II.1
The "oceanic" experience

Aside from unusual modifications of self-perception such as auto-scopy or astral sensations, the most interesting and consistent unconventional change in our self-perception is that known as "oceanic experience." In this condition, so far as its content can be verbalized, the strong sense of distinction between I and not-I is summarily suspended, and with it a number of normal classificatory processes involving categories, boundaries and distinctions, so that all which is perceived is, as it were, incorporated into the I of the perceiver, or the I of the perceiver becomes fused with some experienced totality, according to taste. It is the non-experience of normal categories, rather than any ineffable content, and the fact that it reflects the activity of a nonverbal experiential mode, which makes the "oceanic" experience difficult to verbalize, but judging from the reports of subjects in almost all cultures and periods it is a consistent phenomenon, whether spontaneous or pursued, and whether in-duced by religious exercise, drugs, ordeals, sensory deprivation, or neurological malfunction. It is one of the two unconventional changes in I-perception which humans have actively sought to produce for its own satisfactions and for its consequences in terms of their religious or philosophical world picture (the other is "posses-sion," of which more later). In fact, a very large number of persons in all periods have devoted great energy to the attempt either to experience oceanic sensations or to recapture them once they have been experienced.

In yogic and spontaneous experiences of nondifference, the I simply ceases to obtrude. Under other circumstances it is described as disappearing, as it were, through incorporation into the (external) Deity who is being ardently desired, meditated on, or pursued with prayer. In the Christian tradition male mystics describe this as being "caught up into heaven" (hence "rapture"—the experience is that to which we owe the word) female mystics verbalize the state of nondifference in more nearly sexual terms. For Nārada meditating upon Kṛṣṇa, ecstasy made it impossible to experience both the deity and I-ness at the same time:

> *premātibhara nirbhinna*
> *pulākaṅgo' tinirvṛtaḥ*
> *ānanda-samplave līno*
> *nāpaśyam ubhayaṁ mune*

"Filled with extreme love, my bodily parts overwhelmed with bliss, absorbed in an ocean of rapture, I could not see both [God and myself]."[10]

This is one of the differences between mystical experience pure and religion: religion at once starts to interpret—he who begins with *bhaktī* or the adoration of the Virgin and gets an oceanic experience will combine the two and start building religious constructs thereon. The force of the mystical ecstasis and the component of "bliss," which, by its problem-solving phylogeny we intuit as connoting rightness or truth, reinforce the attitudes with which the devotee started—in fact, it is the "bliss" component which becomes objectified as deity.

One tends to think of this particular modification of the I-experience as occurring spontaneously, like an aura, or as being induced by prolonged and arduous practice. In fact, larval forms of it occur with surprising ease in susceptible people: Deikman[11], whose subjects meditated in an unsophisticated setting on an un-numinous object (a blue vase) without any assistance from religious background, supportive environment, or other sources of potent suggestion, remarks on "the ease and rapidity with which the phenomena were produced. . . . In less than half an hour, phenomena occurred that in other contexts have been described as depersonalization, hallucination, delusion or visual distortion." One feature was loss of differentiation between ego and object. There were no oceanic states—these are indeed usually theoleptic or the result of hard work—but the preliminary condition, I-less perception, which is on the way to the *samprajñāta samādhi* of Patañjali, is apparently producible without elaborate cultural apparatus. There exists, accordingly, a particular state of mind, relatively easily hit upon when one has the knack, in which perception continues but with the homuncular experience of the Self as perceiver in abeyance. A vast amount has been written about this by occultists and very little by neurologists, but its structure is critical to our understanding of "homuncularity," and the fact that it occurs or can be learned, biofeedback fashion, is important to our understanding of the development of human ideas, since the experience is both impressive and reorientating while being difficult to communicate discursively.

"Oceanic experience" is the hallmark not of "religion" but of the mystic: a mystic is one who has or seeks oceanic experiences.[12] In this experience, spontaneous or cultivated, the discursively-minded seer has a vivid conviction of personal identity with, or more correctly nondistinction from, some monistic ground of spiritual and general reality, identified by him according to the theology of his culture. It is a neurological experience with an intense affect of comprehension and bliss.

I and That

Although mystics themselves tend to view the oceanic experience, not very surprisingly, as a positive state, one could equally argue that it is rather an interruption of the convention, or illusion, manifested in the more usual, homuncular, mode of self-experience—it is not oceanic perception which is turned on, but I-ness of the everyday kind which is turned off: in it, conation is suspended either because it seems irrelevant or because it is no longer possible, and adepts who remain in an oceanic state for any length of time have to be tended and have food pushed down their throats. In this respect it superficially resembles catatonia, but only superficially. It can happen at any age, completely unbidden—Agehananda Bharati first experienced it at the age of twelve, and his subsequent career as a Hindu monk was a result of this discovered capacity, not a cause of it. Yet a high proportion of religio-magical exercises in many cultures have the production or recapture of this capacity to turn off or modify prosaic I-ness as their leading object. The aim or knack of yoga is at root nonconceptual (*nirvīkalpa*) or I-less perception. The insight which sees it as a rupture of the veil of illusion seems basically correct: the conventional barrier between self and environment is, in oceanic states, temporarily removed, and the I ceases to be experienced as separate, though it remains active as experiencer of the unconventional situation.

Mystical or ecstatic modifications in I-experience bear a certain resemblance, judging from the literature, to longevity, in that those who practice either give elaborate recipes for inducing something which may well be largely innate, though it can be fostered by suitable sādhana given the appropriate constitutional makeup. Altered I-states are morally neutral for reasons unrelated to philosophy—the seer is altered by them to the extent that he or she normally appropriates experience. Bharati (op. cit.) remarks that a person who was a stinker before his ecstatic experience will usually be a stinker after it. In the same way artificial dissociators of normal I-ness produce disparate effects in different people—not all LSD experiences involve oceanic experience, or bliss, or, indeed, anything in particular. Seers, mystics and shamans are accordingly people in whom this type of I-modification occurs easily. They may cultivate it, or it may cultivate them. In a culture with few strong religious sentiments they may not see their experiences as "religious" even if they cultivate them (any more than practitioners of sexual koinonia now see it as religious): in religiocentric cultures they make the religious noises appropriate to the culture, and incorporate their visionary activities with them, as did St Teresa or Ramakrishna. Ecstatic experience, even in cultures like the Eskimo who make great use of it, or those where psychedelics are ritually employed, is probably in all human societies confined to a minority, though this may be a sizeable minority. On the other hand it seems to occur spontaneously in all cultures including our own, and it constantly contributes to systematized religion as the continuous rain of meteorites increases the mass of the Earth, its contribution being a continual reopening of the question of I-ness as against That—most prominent in the religious philosophy of cultures which most cultivate I-changing experiences.

Theistic mysticism, both Christian and Vaiṣnava, is *dvaita* as it were by expectation. The image is often that of the Self as feminine, regardless of the biological sex of the mystic, "going forth by night to meet her lover." This situation, known in Sanskrit as the *abhisārikā rāsa*, is a favorite in Indian painting and poetry. Its prime focus is the story of Radha and the other *gopīs*, married ladies all, going out by night in total abandon and defiance of convention to seek Kṛṣna, but it is repeated in exact detail by St John of the Cross in the splendid poem upon which *The Ascent of Mount Carmel* is a commentary. The complete oceanic experience with fusional suppression of identity is here equated with feminine orgasm as a transient experience which gives rise to a divine relationship. It is striking to contrast the spontaneity and impulsion of this experience expressed in poetry with the labor of self-suppression and the ascetic rejection of all sensory and spontaneous experience (vairagya, indifference) counsel-led both by conventional Vaiṣnava mystics and by St John in his treatise for aspirants, where vairagya is to be attained by mortification and a kind of serial amputation of the self. This is the mysticism of the sensual who have rejected sensuality. Among other Christian mystics the experience brings less conflict: in Meister Eckhart and the author of the *Cloud of Unknowing* the fusional experience is directly addressed. Women mystics—St Teresa or Julian of Norwich—seem to address both dvaita and advaita states within their theological beliefs but with less anxiety, less need for protective clothing. Both the *Song of Songs*, which was St John's model, and the Kṛṣna saga referred originally to a secular sexuality deeply disturbing to the renounced of either tradition. The relation of asceticism to this anxiety cannot be overlooked. It is not the whole story, but it patterns the mystic's injunction of self-denial.

In St John of the Cross one senses an overwhelming experience, the "bliss" of Indian writers, which was both spontaneous and highly disturbing, leaving us wondering whether he can in fact have climbed Mount Carmel in the leaden boots which he prescribes to his students. The intensity of the lasting results, in devotion and religious conviction, was equally overwhelming. Yet structurally similar oceanic experiences, often quite unbidden, appear to be far from uncommon in people who are neither monks by vocation nor deeply religious—the intensity and the devotional use are in the man, not in the experience. One can imagine that a physicist might apply them not to union with God but to a perception of universal structure, while others derive from them simply a comforting conviction of meaning and of coherence, rather as Julian of Norwich, having held the Universe in her hand and found it no larger than a nut, acquired the conviction that "all shall be well, and all manner of things shall be well." Some religious people—Thomas Merton is a leading example—require considerable reinforcement from the apparatus of monastic or ecclesiastical sādhana to achieve an oceanic experience: Merton's later acquaintance with Zen masters and with Quakers gave him an insight into the surprising generality of oceanic states as a human potential. The intellectual, sacramental or other use which is made of them depends on the person to whom, and the system of belief in which, they occur.

Hardy[13] set out to examine the religious experience of those in modern British culture who had any, and who volunteered its content in their own words. The descriptions were of two related experiences—that of an external "superhuman force which makes for righteousness," and the experiential fusion, *dvaita* or *advaita*, of the mystical tradition:

> "It seemed to me that in some way I was extending into my surroundings and was becoming one with them. At the same time I felt a sense of lightness, exhilaration and power as if I was beginning to understand the true meaning of the whole universe."

> "I have a growing sense of reality and personal identity which comes from being united to something more powerful than myself. . . ."

> ". . . it seems to be outside of me and enormous yet at the same time I am part of it—everything is. . . ."

Others describe *satori*-like sensations of joy and "rightness" not basically fusional (identity is not suppressed) in which natural objects and events appear in heightened colors ("lit up from inside").

Hardy does not in this place give the incidence of such experiences in the 4,000 records he collected, but it appears to have been quite high. All were derived from cultures (chiefly Britain, but also Australia, New Zealand and the USA) where mystical experience is not an overt goal of established religion; they were however volunteered as religious, not secular or pathological, together with statements of Christian faith and typical conversional experiences which are conventionally religious—those who had the experiences perceived them to be of a religious nature. All were spontaneous or theoleptic; none of those quoted were conditioned by yoga or psychedelic agents, but all are recognizable modes of the mystical experience.

Mystics, because their experiences are profoundly important to them, tend to dislike psychiatric approaches. We do have, however, to look at the "psychopathology" of oceanic states, if they have one, not to deflate their philosophical interest but simply to find out how they occur. Contact with the psychedelic cult has brought them to medical notice as real events. In a climate of enthusiasm for Oriental religion and meditation they may conceivably occur, or be volunteered, more often. In view of the damaging effects of "schizophrenia" and "hallucination" as labels, the differential diagnosis is important. Very few career mystics of any persuasion, and very few individuals who have had one or more oceanic experiences spontaneously, are clinically psychotic by any intelligible criteria, but many psychotics engage in cult formation based on hallucinatory experiences. A careful history will usually discriminate psychotic experiences, which almost always contain persistent thought disorder, from oceanic states which mimic them in language. Alarming inspiration of recent onset should be viewed with suspicion, and sudden alterations of consciousness require neurological and EEG examination, but to the clinician who is aware of oceanic states as a phenomenon the possessor of the genuine variety does not sound in any way psychotic, even when the content of his experiences renders him unconventional—there is no thought disorder and no blunting of affect, though there may be loss of interest in mundane concerns: naive spontaneous oceanics in a culture which does not offer an institutional religious context may embrace bizarre or cranky cult affiliations which do. Whether unbidden oceanic states represent an idiosyncrasy of brain function is another matter—if they do, so probably does musical genius, which can lead to equally striking effects on values and lifestyle. These considerations are important because of the tendency of the culture to medicalize values and label any incomprehensible behavior as psychotic: the doctor is accordingly caught between diagnosing a psychosis which is not there, and missing one which is, since both mistakes can gravely injure the patient.

Clearcut oceanic states actually present fewer problems in diagnostics than do some other religious experiences. Consider the following history:

> A 33-year-old American housewife of Fundamentalist background had lapsed from Christian affiliation. While working in a library she suddenly found herself unable to write normally, and found that "foreign handwriting came from the tip of my pen," which repeatedly wrote "John and Barbara, I have come to help you," John being her husband. Within a few days the phenomenon spread to several relatives and friends, causing great alarm and fear of impending insanity. In succeeding periods the possessional phenomena were replaced by an "inner voice," a striking increase in vividness and perception of detail in external objects, including

taste and smell, and an experience of premonitory tension—
anxious before disastrous world events and beatific before
pleasant ones. The experience of the original disciples in this
sequence of events led to close bonding between them, a shared
conviction that the existence of God had been demonstrated, the
making of further converts who came, sometimes to their own
surprise, to share in the unusual experiences, and the creation of a
small Bible-reading cult centered in the "inner voice." One
convert took to writing poetry, and all found the "inner voice" a
reliable source of counsel in personal problems.

This series of events was unusual in being epidemic: if it had been
volunteered as a solitary experience it would have done very well for
the onset of a psychotic episode: as it is, the writer shows no thought
disorder, no blunting of affect, and is not hallucinated. The "inner
voice" of the group is recognized as internal although it is given
spiritual significance, and is no more hallucinatory than the Quaker
Inner Light or the Vicar's conviction of guidance. Only the
possessional automatic writing is out of culture. How an element of
Haitian possessionalism got into a Biblical Fundamentalist is
unclear: it sounds like an echo of nineteenth-century ouija-board
spiritism incorporated into an eclectic conversion-experience. Many
conversional experiences both in previously religious and previously
areligious persons can be extremely odd. Luckily for psychiatry they
are more often valued than complained of, because anthropological as
well as psychoanalytic experience is needed to make sense of them and
distinguish them from the equally unusual but basically destructive or
unproductive experiences of the psychotic.

In a culture which cultivates oceanic experiences they are
actively sought, not complained of to the doctor. If, as seems
extremely likely, the tendency to have such experiences is an
independently distributed variable, some "mystics" will suffer from
psychotic or other illnesses, rather as some will be left-handed, and
they, rather than the normal bulk of the sample, will fall into the
hands of the psycho-statistician. In fact, if we exclude aura-like
phenomena associated with the epilepsies, oceanic experience is not a
common concomitant of any mental illness unless, like some enragé
nineteenth-century rationalists, we label anyone who seeks religiously tinted experiences which are out of the ordinary as being for
that reason a little touched. Spiritism and occultism, which do
produce and have produced a very odd fauna of dissociative
personalities, probably added to this impression. Janet and Briquet
probably never met an Indian or Japanese sadhu in the clinical
setting: European spontaneous mystics, in spite of Steiner and
Ouspensky, usually either kept quiet about it or belonged to
contemplative orders of religious where the phenomenon did not
seem so odd.

Textbooks of psychiatry commonly discuss oceanic states in the context of psychosis. They are not, however, a usual manifestation, at least of schizophrenia: schizophrenics may have a variety of odd mental experiences, but "oceanic" sensations are less common than in temporal lobe epilepsy, especially when it affects the dominant hemisphere, or in so-called "anxiety-bliss psychosis," which may have more relation to migraine than to schizophrenia. The suggestion that schizophrenics were the mystics of primitive society has little to support it: shamans not infrequently appear psychotic, but the repertoire of these tolerated-disturbed individuals does not usually include oceanic or meditative states so much as hallucinatory voices and experiences. Like other dislocations of body image, notably autoscopic hallucinations, spontaneous oceanic states appear to be benign and show little correlation with psychosis even when they appear to arise from transient or intermittent brain dysfunction. The psychopathology of career mystics is another matter, and in any case not over-relevant to this argument. Allowance being made for belief and for culture norms, it is difficult to know without examining the patient whether brain dysfunction in a given person is causing unusual experiences, or whether unusual experiences are encouraging unconventional behavior. St Francis, Ramakrishna and Blake were all rated insane by conventional contemporaries and inspired by later generations. Some oceanic states can look like catatonia, but the resemblance stops there. The analogy to drug-induced experiences is closer, but hallucinogens only appear to produce oceanic experiences in susceptible people, and the effect is nonspecific as well as being heavily influenced by expectation and milieu. Defining an oceanic state as one in which the subject experiences bliss, nondifference from That and suspended I-ness, not many psychiatrists will have seen a case, nor will it usually be presented as a complaint.

The oceanic adept in a culture which accepts his activity as valuable may be highly rational and conventional—Ramana Maharshi, for example, or St Teresa—though some of these individuals will have gone through a period of acute anxiety and disorganization early in life not very dissimilar from the *"Trema"* of incipient schizophrenia, followed by an intense period of struggle, which may include what sound like dissociative or catatonic episodes. Ramana Maharshi's career began with a sudden, overwhelming fear of death at the age of sixteen, followed by an intuition of enlightenment: but for others a vivid oceanic experience may occur without any premonitory brooding or disturbance and be accepted as a matter of course—the difference seems to depend on the personality of the individual, not the correlates of an oceanic experience per se. In Ramana Maharshi's case, which would pass for an example of so-called "anxiety-bliss psychosis," the son of a mystically-inclined and very orthodox Smārta Brahmin family encountered oceanic experience in the middle of a conversion-type crisis, rather as Jesus and Gautama discovered a religious "identity" during a period of withdrawal and search, but many other persons have had oceanic experiences under prosaic conditions without making religious capital from them or adhering to a system in which repetitions of the experience are cultivated. William James, for example, had a vivid oceanic experience while "in the wilderness," not on a retreat but on a camping expedition, and enjoyed it for what it was. Prolonged solitude is an archaic facilitator for unusual mental experiences which most urban humans do not undergo. The experience itself looks like a trick or manner of mental activity more easily provoked in some people than in others, but probably latent in many people without any pathological association. The typical "praecox feeling" is extremely rare in career mystics, but extremely common in possessional shamans.

II.2
Oceanic perception as alternative

These results suggest that fusional experiences, so far from being confined to those who pursue them by artificial means, or to cultures which overtly value them, are a reasonably common happening. They are probably commoner than Hardy's results would imply, in that sceptics, while impressed by them, are less likely to report them in religious terms. Whether they are commoner in those who actively seek them is arguable; some of the Indian mystics interviewed by Bharati[12] give the impression that spiritual exercises are what they do because such exercises are expected of them and occupy the intervals between spontaneous fusional states: others appear to have the ability to "go critical" at will, though the theory of their disciples that they are in constant samādhi is incompatible with the nature of the experience. Throughout mystical literature one finds a certain indignation among professional saints that certain sinners, or at least laymen, have spontaneous experiences without effort—on the basis that nothing which occurs so easily can be the genuine article. A similar feeling of jealousy underlies the hostility of "straight" mystics to identical experiences brought on by drugs. Of the four experiences chronicled by Bharati himself, two were wholly unprovoked, one followed Tantrik initiation involving ritualized sex, and one a combination of sex and LSD-25. Of these, then, only one was induced by a traditional method.

Exceptional states of mind are not all of "religion," but their commonness and striking character suggest they are an important component in its formation, and they pertain always to identity. Their intellectual importance in a modern setting is that whether spontaneous, generated by spiritual exercises, or by hallucinogens, they puncture and radically reorder our conventional world-perception. This is, in fact, a perception based on a concept of objectivity which is itself culturally acquired and goes with a particular cultural style—that which has produced experimental and inductive science, and which leans heavily on analogies drawn from the machine. This cultural style influences, for example, the way we experience the body image—the body being a "machine" requiring expert servicing, and, when ailing, a technological fix—and the world image—"nature" being a machine-like system susceptible to fixing in the same way when its regularities conflict with short-term objectives. We shall here, in fact, be using a machine-derived model—that of systems theory—to suggest a model for the neural origins of the I experience. The use of abstraction to elucidate structure accordingly has its uses. What oceanic states provide to the product of our cultural tradition, rather than that of the Hindu or the prephilosophical traditions, is the ability to perceive an alternative approach to structure and a supplementary rather than a competing paradigm of experience. This complementarity might well prove to be a new cultural mix, and to inaugurate a new, or a radically modified, style. It also has striking implications at the purely discursive level by enabling us to experience the degree to which the "objective" macrocosm is in fact being patterned by the idiosyncrasy of our sense of identity.

In fact, if in the past the potentiality for this kind of acategorical perception was religion-forming and conducive of pantheism, for us it is religion-disturbing. We do not ordinarily recognize the predominantly logical mode which our culture has adopted since the eighteenth century as "religious," but the oceanic experience is disruptive of a learned behavior if only by making it conscious through contrast with a different perception. In forming our cultural style, as Mumford says,

> the process of mechanization was furthered by an ideology that gave absolute precedence and cosmic authority to the machine itself. When an ideology conveys such universal meanings and commands such obedience, it has become, in fact, a religion, and its imperatives have the dynamic force of myth. . . . From the nineteenth century on, this refurbished religion united thinkers of the most diverse temperaments, backgrounds and superficial

beliefs: minds as different as Marx and Ricardo, Carlyle and Mill, Comte and Spenser, subscribed to its doctrines; and from the beginning of the nineteenth century on, the working classes, finding themselves helpless to resist these new forces, countered the capitalist and militarist expressions of this myth with myths of their own—those of socialism, anarchism, or communism—under which the machine would be exploited, not for a ruling elite, but for the benefit of the proletarian masses. Against this machine-conditioned utopia only a handful of heretics, mostly poets and artists, dared to hold out.[14]

Anything with which I experience myself as fully continuous cannot easily be analogized as a machine, because a machine is by definition a not-I to be addressed by manipulation. Moreover however illusional the nondifference experienced in oceanic states, they tend to create a profound impression because of their unusual and compelling character: in other words, their effects last, as a reservation on the completeness of the way in which we normally experience and analogize experience. For those already provided with a theology, they are interpreted within it to give a sense of revelation or superior insight which can carry a disabling sense of conviction; for the more open minded, they are simply revealing experiences, which cast doubt on the inevitability of usual modes of experiencing Self and Other. Moreover during or in association with them the acategorical experience may itself acquire patterning (into intuitions of symmetry, fourfoldness, continual sequence and regression, or the like). These are aura-like, or dream-like, in being almost impossible to seize upon and verbalize, but they carry their own conviction of rightness, and insofar as they are verbalized they show rather high consistency regardless of the culture of the subject and the means used to induce the oceanic state. Clearly what is being introspected here is some feature of the structure of the perceptual mechanism or the zero-input display of the human brain, but a high proportion of the magical and religious systems which emphasize symmetry and attribute power to various geometric structures, either as literal symbols or as abstract antitheses, coincide rather closely with the contentless symmetries perceived during oceanic suspension of I-ness by mystics or by subjects who have taken hallucinogens. It is in the nature of discourse that we cannot be convincingly discursive about wholly internal structures, but this is probably as close as we can come to being so on a basis of introspection alone.

There is no *a priori* reason why "religion," or for that matter "philosophy," should imply exclusive dogmatism, but empirically they commonly do. There are, or rather have been, two exclusivist views, one championing each of the two possible modes of perception. Hinduism, Buddhism and other philosophies based on a high experiential contact with oceanic experience regard that manner of perceiving "reality" as the Truth, and the conventional mode as "illusion." Science and commonsense regard the world we see as basically "real," even if some of its fine structure requires special techniques of demonstration, and above all as consistent, with the corollary that verificatory science is both the only way we can get intelligible information about "the real" and our only defense against the human capacity for arbitrary hypothesis—"story-telling." This point of view has been beautifully put by Medawar[15], who contrasts scientism with poeticism. It has to be noticed, however, that what Medawar is attacking is not "oceanic experience," which is an observation, whatever its significance, but woolly minded theorizing and the creation of wholly literary models which, since they can neither be tested nor refuted, amount simply to puff pastry. He picks cocksure psychoanalysis as a prime model of this kind, and it deserves much of the criticism if we look at published literature. Freud's original research, however, was not antiscientific—his basic premise was that human irrationalities are not arbitrary but biologically structured, often round distortions of the curious process by which what will later be expressed as sexuality appears to be displaced into childhood, far ahead of its eventual expression in reproduction. What stymied his highly scientific and hardnosed inclination to deal in neurology and biology and those languages alone was that neither was at that time sufficiently advanced to tackle the program: accordingly he did not publish his elegant systems model of the neural basis of psychology (it has only recently been published by Karl Pribram) and settled for clinical application. In the event his clinical observations have turned out to be more instructive than curative, and more relevant to primatology than the cure of mental disease. Some of his followers, provided with a total explanatory system, and backed by the real observation that uncovering of neotenic attitudes in the adult is disturbing and leads to "resistance," made hay without intellectual scruple, and it is these that Medawar rightly castigates. He is equally hard, and just as rightly hard, on softheaded poeticizing about Truth and the Deeper Reality. Deeper Realities are something in which not-quite-first-rate minds wallow and eventually drown: ordinary, shallow Reality presents quite sufficient interest to the sceptical and unself-indulgent.

But this is not what the "religious" difference between objectivist and introspectivist is about. It is, indeed, of quite a different order. The Hindu does not give a row of beans for poetic Deeper Reality—he has observed that there is a state of mind obtainable by accident or by application in which perception is altered in such a way that ordinary perceptions are seen to be contingent. That in itself would hardly bother the scientist in the objectivist tradition, though the Hindu did not get where he is by considering that a chair or an apple are local aggregations of energy rather than "objects." But neither should he be bothered by the less naive conclusion that the structures which we perceive, whether directly by looking at them, or indirectly by inference and experimentation, are determined at least as much by the cerebral apparatus which performs the acts of perception and inference as by structure present in the inputs we examine. Physics has already reached this conclusion by examining the results it has obtained. Where the Hindu experimentalist differs from the particle physicist is in the experiential insight which comes from turning off some of the habitual process of analysis—on a basis of this, the Hindu experimentalist overstates his case and regards the entire product of conventional observation as merely illusory, and conventional categories as artefactual as against "reality."

With this overstatement the scientist ought to have some sympathy, in that oceanic bumptiousness is the counterpart of the bumptiousness of discovery. Science itself has always had a hard time in transcending the intuitive, from the "flat earth" on. The farther we pursue physics or neuropsychology or both, the more evident it becomes that the kind of universe we see as objective depends as much on the system which is doing the seeing as on what is there to be seen, but we continue to be intuitive about our perceptions even when we know that the earth is an oblate spheroid. Over a large part of practical application, the intuitive–verificatory model works. For these purposes—and science is a practical activity—argument about how far our perceptions of fossils, influenza viruses or comets are "real" is merely diversionary, like a denial that terrestrial surfaces are flat when one is laying tiles. Higher physics, which is where the shoe really begins to pinch, is buffered against naive intuitivism by recourse to mathematics: the fact that we can now live with a far more subjective and "illusory" universe is in itself a rousing tribute to the efficacy of the scientific method. Groddeck thought that psychoanalysis could never work because humans were incapable of overcoming their built-in biases and identifying them. The fact that we have got to the insight which the yogi obtains by direct perception through our own method of rational induction indicates the force of the inductive method. But it would not hurt us to have the direct perception as well. This is the answer to the question whether a mere change in state of mind can impart worthwhile intellectual content. Freud, as a hardnosed objectivist, replied that it could not, and that oceanic experiences were probably not worth investigating, except as evidences of malfunction. But the correct answer has to be yes, if the alteration involves a critical insight into the way we habitually process information. What we now need is rational investigation of the mind as a perceptive and analytic system, and if odd experiences throw light on this, they are a source of information too.

There is a nice Indian story of the junior mystic who was cultivating oceanic experience by meditating in the middle of a road, when a man rushed passed shouting "Run! Here comes a runaway elephant!" The yogi, however, stuck to his theoretical position. Saying to himself "The elephant and I are nondifferent, for both are Brahman," he sat his ground, and the elephant trod on him. Visited by his guru in hospital he received what is vulgarly termed a rocket: "Idiot!" said the swami, "why did you not run?"

"Because, swami-ji, you taught me, and I know, that the elephant and I are nondifferent, categories are illusory, and the beast too is Brahman!"

"Yes, you fool," said the swami, "but so was the mahout who told you to get out of the way."

In other words, there is a time and a place for everything. In dealing with elephants, and macrosystems generally, the intuitive view works. Over most of science overanalysis of mental process and lack of confidence in the consistent behavior of an objective world generate mystification, not insight, and we were lucky not to have got involved with oceanic perception at a time when it could have played old Harry with the useful development of objective science. But we are big boys now, and confronted with the odd behavior of quarks and the occurrence of particle events in which effect appears to precede cause, we need to cultivate any available technologies, including archaic ones, which might throw light on our most important instrument of observation, the homuncular convention and the human classificatory method which goes with it. From now on there are not two hostile ideologies of "reality" but one continuous and internally consistent project. Scientists will probably go on regarding "mystics" as poetic but unregenerate story-tellers, and conventional Hindus will go on regarding the renewed Western interest in acategorical perception as one more attempt to reduce spirituality to materialist terms, but in this case events will simply knock their heads together. Science in its Western form will go on practicing its own sādhana—as it should—but it might gain an unexpected set of resources from a sceptical study of Indian and Buddhist philosophy: from the original texts, one might add, and not from itinerant swamis who peddle Oriental "spirituality" and market it in mottoes out of fortune cookies. "Spirituality," whatever that may be, has nothing to do with epistemology, and probably little to do with religion, unless it means sensitivity to, and integrity in dealing with, experience: and that science, or at least good science, already has.

Practicing "mystics" may or may not be interested in the ontological significance of their experiences. Faced with an unusual and deeply impressive experience, whether it happens to be samādhi or being the sole survivor of an air crash, one would naturally attempt

to integrate it into one's customary world view. If the experiencer is a
career religionist, he or she will religionize it: the pantheistic authors
of the Upaniṣads saw the fusional aspect of oceanic states as
experiential evidence for pantheism, whereas Martin Buber, who
had had similar experiences, saw them as confirming the unity of his
own "self." Prof. Zaehner infers that there is more than one type of
oceanic experience, a not-pukka variety (including that induced by
drugs) which is merely enthusiastic, and a pukka variety which is
genuinely religious and incorporates an objective God in the
Christian tradition without presuming to become part of Him. One is
tempted to say, in the words of a celebrated lady, "Well, he would,
wouldn't he?" Within Hinduism the same kind of ontological dispute
has gone on for centuries between Śaiva and Vedanta-type mystics
and Vaiṣnava dualists. "Touching their differences, only Allah at the
Day of Resurrection shall decide between them."

   This is not a book about theories of existence, Absolute
Grounds, or for that matter Gods. I am profoundly interested in the
ontological implications of unusual states of mind not as ammunition
for theology but because they might possibly throw light on the
properties of an instrument with which all scientists work, namely
the human brain. Science, however, is itself by way of being a
"religion" based on one particular version of the human way-of-
seeing: for it, other ways-of-seeing do have practical and possibly
revisionist consequences, and it is this possibility which makes
oceanic states more than a curiosity. One has to listen carefully to
what different religious traditions go on to say about oceanic
experience, however bizarre that is, because the structures which
they erect on it might quite possibly throw light on what, cerebrally,
is going on. In this context the more naive and "superstitious" the
interpretation, the more likely it is to be onto something other than
purely intellectual soufflé-making—vision-inspired cosmologies, for
example, make sense when we apply them to the way an objectivized
world comes into existence *for us*, not to astronomical objects. At the
same time, so impressive is the contrast between an oceanic
perception, even if brief, and conventional linear perception, and so
old is the record of such states in human history, that they are bound
to have been formative of human ideas to an extent quite out of
proportion to their frequency. So long as science was dealing with
phenomena where objectivist approximation worked, or could be
boosted to work by adding, for example, non-Euclidean geometries,
this kind of comparative study might have been a rather demoralizing
luxury. Today, however, both a crop of apparent epistemological
paradoxes over the meaning we attach to the idea of "existence" in
physics, and a radical revision of our ideas about the way the brain
processes and transduces data, make it an obligatory and possibly a
productive exercise.

The Democritean model of a universe consisting of discrete "things"—with its consequence that if any structure is found to have components, these must be identified until an irreducible "thing" is discovered—has had wide utility in areas such as atomic chemistry, the periodic table and finally particle physics. Its universal adoption by science as against field theories represents a victory for the commonsense or conventionally based model derived from normal categories of experience. It was also largely an accidental choice, made because it did indeed chime with easily visualized models. Alternative models were to hand in European philosophy since Pythagoras, but they were obscured by the lack of practical consequences, especially in Platonic idealism (Plato has a lot to answer for) and later by the revolt of philosophy against theological attempts to rationalize allegorical concepts by means of double-speak. Moreover the convention of discrete "things" did in hindsight provide a discipline within which science could operate; at any time before the present a thingless universe would have provided a hunting license for precisely the kind of intellectual puff-pastry-making which Medawar identifies as antiscientific. A thingless universe could indeed have been hypothecated at almost any time since the beginnings of Greek philosophy and certainly at any time since Pythagoras, and sometimes was, long before Bishop Berkeley, but there was simply not the mathematical or physical knowledge to prop up a hypothesis of this kind as more than an intuition; especially since in interpreting macrosystems such as molecules, when science finally became experimental, its convenience as a convention is low compared with atomism. The only justification for the intuition would lie in a direct experience of thingless perception; this might be impressive to the philosopher who had the experience, but is not ontological evidence: like St Bernadette's conversation with the Blessed Virgin, it might reinforce existing beliefs but would not impress career sceptics.

European philosophy was in fact far more widely exposed to the "thingless" or field-theory models of reality which we now think of as Oriental than has been recognized, among Stoics in particular. Zeno's father travelled widely and brought him Oriental books, Pythagoras probably visited Persia and India, several later Stoics were based in areas of the Middle East which traded continuously with India at the height of its Buddhist period, and even Seneca wrote his doctoral thesis on Indian cultural anthropology. Certainly from the time of Alexander on, Greek philosophy had extensive access to Buddhism and pre-Buddhist Hinduism. King Menander in Northern India (the "Milinda" of the Pali *Milindapanha*) conducted Socratic dialogues with Nagasena which are familiar to most Buddhists but to virtually no European Hellenists.

It was a signal dispensation of Providence, so far as science was concerned, that the Greek sense of practicality, which separated charismatic aspects of philosophy from brass-tacks applications such as mathematics, the Greek zest for life, which was highly inimical to "detachment," Buddhist-style, and the Greek distrust of Oriental exoticism generally, made the illusory character of experience an unpopular philosophical postulate. Even the submersion of the Graeco–Roman world in Christianity kept sensory reality real—the world might be evil but it was not virtual or illusory, except perhaps for the Gnostics. Where field-theory models based on meditative experiences did find a foothold, they carried along with them superstructures such as pantheism rather than a literal comment on physics. Moreover for Greeks, Stoics included, philosophy was closely involved with ethics and citizenship. Diogenes might secede to live in a tub, but he did so in the marketplace. There were no Greek anchorites. On the other side, Buddhist and later Hindu philosophers for their part were not overconcerned with the significance of *maya* for physics. Some, like Nagarjuna, developed their own quasi-Platonic system to explain where categorical perceptions were "stored" in consciousness, but if the result of introspection was direct contact with an Absolute, why bother with the structural regularities of mere appearances? One must suspect that the antithesis between the "spiritual" Orient and the "materialistic" or practical West is a lot older than Mme Blavatsky; it is already present in the making-over of Buddhist ideas by Stoicism—if indeed that is where they came from—and the replacement of mere self-edification by ethics, demonstration, and the practical concerns of Hellenistic city-state citizenship.

If Christianity had been more guiltlessly introspective and less modeled by the external God of Judaism and the Alexandrine ambivalence toward the Flesh—which pulled in different directions, but both against the validation of do-it-yourself ontological mysticism—we might never have got objectivizing science. As it was, even medieval disputes over transubstantiation, however much they turned on "essences," dealt with the objective—real bread into real flesh. From this brew superstition and science crystallized out as polar opposites. A Gnostic church might have produced yogis, but never science or technology. Oceanic experience went on occurring among contemplatives, but with a theological safety net under it. We may feel, with historical hindsight, that it was practically fortunate Greece had career philosophers but no career Brahmins. The other major benefactor of rationalist science was the Devil, of whom we will speak later on: his contribution was to deflate the credibility of all spontaneous ecstatic experiences.

Between the end of the Middle Ages and the founding of the Royal Society, serious European science did in fact wobble dangerously between internal and external observation: the conflict of agendas can be seen in alchemy. We can infer what might have happened to science if the premature introspectionists had prevailed from the Teilhardian mishmash in the works of highly talented and experimentally minded men like Michael Maier or John Dee. The ferment of emancipation from Roman dogmatism was in many ways like that of the present-day psychedelic and esoteric revolt against "square" society and technological science—the "Rosicrucians" who congregated round the short-lived Bohemian court of the Elector Frederick were in revolt against Catholic orthodoxy and in favor of trying everything—chemistry, geometry, mathematics, occultism, Pythagorean field theories based on music, numerology, the Cabbala, and the "Egyptian" texts of Hermes Trismegistus. Much of this now makes sense in the hindsight of experimental science, Jungian psychology, and Orientalist studies, but it was a heady brew at any time. Only pot and LSD were missing. The second of these, however, had been otherwise occupied elsewhere. Throughout the Middle Ages, spoiled rye with toxic and occasionally psychedelic properties had been a contributor to several epidemics of demonomania. Both Protestants and Catholics were acutely aware of demonic activity, which they attributed to their ecclesiastical opponents, to dissentients generally, and to wizards and alchemical speculators in particular, especially when otherwise heretical. Many major contributors to mathematics and science, including Descartes, Kepler, Leibnitz, and pre-eminently Newton, were intensely interested in this ferment of speculation—Descartes himself may just possibly have owed his philosophical emphasis on I-ness to some kind of oceanic experience—but they prudently confined their public utterances to more materialistic and less explosive matters and to mathematics. The imaginary "invisible college" of Rosicrucian mystics, combining evangelical Christianity with empirical science and Pythagorean theory, gave place to the real and experimental Royal Society: if an accident of history had placed natural hallucinogens on the side of the sages rather than of the Devil, there is no knowing what might have come of it. What did in fact come of it was that oceanic states from this source were attributed to the Devil, oceanic states in the context of organized religion to the religious framework in question, and if mathematicians or philosophers happened to encounter them as a source of new ideas they prudently kept quiet about it. Nobody can now consider this outcome as other than fortunate. The popular mythology and the religious dogma of the times attributed *all* non-duty-paying states of altered consciousness not to "vision" but to possession, and since, as with drug trips, the influence of expectation is a major factor in shaping what is experienced, possessional–dissociative states, *Exorcist*-style, were for a while admitted to the culture, and have continued to crop up, first in witch trials and later in medical and psychiatric practice.

II.3
Possession

Possession is a very different but equally venerable resource in the manipulation of the experience of identity. In this case, rather than achieving one-ness with That by a suppression of discrete identity, the experience of normal identity yields the controls, and the center stage, to some other component of the internal fauna. Possession in the Judaeo-Christian tradition is another unused resource, and the parts of the inner structure to which control is surrendered are assumed to be negative or demonic on the rare occasions when it occurs, as in spontaneous psychotics.

Possession occurs readily in religious traditions which cultivate it: in most of these, however (the Haitian religions are a good example), the experience is not enlightening to the possessed, though it may conceivably be abreactive. However vividly the possessed person acts out the attributes of the possessing spirit—and Haitian adepts commonly perform extraordinary feats of energy or transformation in expressing the nature of the substitute self—he or she is usually totally, or at least partially, unaware on return to a normal condition of the content of what has been done. Possession as a religious resource is therefore of value not to the possessed but to other members of the cult, for whom the *alter ego* is made actual and can be conversed with in the person of the "horse" upon whom the spirit rides. In possessional cults much of the expertise of the organizing priest lies in facilitating such manifestations, directing them so that an appropriate *alter ego* is placed in control, terminating and controlling the possession if it threatens to get out of hand, and dealing with the occasional case in which neither "horse" nor "*mystère*" can secure the upper hand and injury to normal identity experience appears to threaten. The Haitian *houn'gan* (priest) is also adept at determining by ritual which of a vast pleroma of otherselves should possess an initiate, and which has in fact done so.

The experience is neurologically interesting in that it appears to occur far more easily, with cult encouragement, that the more sophisticated I-modifications of oceanic states, and in the amnesia which appears to follow it. Haitian syncretism has produced a vast list of *loas* capable of becoming manifest in this way—derived from several African traditions, Christian saints, arbitrary personages such as Maître Cimetière or Reine Congo France, together with others who appear to reflect fractionation of the various Jungian otherselves. Even Blake's Four Zoas and their Emanations figure in the Pantheon—Urizen as Danbhala, the cosmic serpent-architect, Tharmas and Enion as Aoueh R Oyo and Erzulie, custodians of water and the Moon, and Luvah as Legba Ati Bon, identified with the Cosmic Tree and the crucified Christ as well as with his African original. The repertoire of structural introspection can apparently be fragmented almost indefinitely to provide subsidiary selves capable of "mounting" or possessing an initiate. In other religious traditions it is the shaman himself who identifies, either theatrically or with genuine identity-suppression, with a force or spirit whose power or attributes he wishes to employ, or whom he wishes to make available for question, appeasement or control. The Haitian *houn'sih* (initiate), however, appears to substitute some other copilot for the normally experienced I purely to dramatize or express its content to others.

III.1
The mechanism of I-ness

So difficult is the homuncular experience to handle that neurophilos-
ophers are forced to attack it by analogy or by way of hypothetical
systems, the most interesting of which is Feigl's "autocerebros-
cope."[16] Imagine that a duplicate, "slave" brain is connected in
parallel with mine, identical in structure and in physiology, and so
wired that every event in my brain is exactly mirrored in the copy. I
have then two sources of observation—what "I" perceive, and what
I see going on in the replica. Argument then proceeds as to the
difference between I-ness experienced and the perceptions of I *in
propria persona*, and I-ness observed, together with the neural events
which make up a perception—on the lines that these differ from the
subjective perception as a picture differs from an experience.

This kind of model is an interesting source of speculation, and
focuses attention on singularities of our self-experience. It is also a
possible way of getting around Goedel (each system contains
elements of information about the other which that other lacks), but
if it really existed it would have properties not allowed for by Feigl—
one being that it would be inherently unstable and would oscillate,
since my perception of my relation to the copy's experience would
immediately show up in the copy, be perceived by me, feed back, and
so on *ad infinitum*. A more interesting and less captious character is
that the body image acts in some limited ways like an "auto-
cerebroscope" in mimicking some but not all of the ongoing activities
of the I. Globus[17] uses the model to show that there cannot be an
ontological identity between mental and neural events, but I have a
feeling that what he really shows is that the extreme oddness of the
way we experience "felt" as against observed experience introduces a
principle of uncertainty, due to a basic contradiction in the model: if
brain 2 (the slave) really did in fact copy every action of brain 1, the
overwhelming likelihood is that it would have I-experience of its
own, and an inherent capacity to observe brain 1. The model implies
that it is the cerebral equivalent of the motorless second car towed
behind a powered trolley, but in this case it is not a replica of all the
aspects of brain 1, and any postulation of an override or one-way
drive creates more contradictions than the model will in any case
carry. I-ness is an illusion and an experience. It can only be
experienced, or inferred from communication, not observed from the
outside, and it subsumes the problem of conation—what sets it off,
whether random variation, a "drive to action," or specific inputs,

where if at all it can be said to be localized, what, neurally, occurs when it operates and I "decide" to move my finger, or to speculate about brain physiology, and a number of other equally intractable but highly important questions. Luckily we do not need to address all of these. The point of raising them is to reiterate the oddness of the self-experience, as well as its centrality in ordering all other human perceptions, and the fact that since if it is not magical or supernatural it must be neural, and neural structures and manners of data handling will accordingly appear both in what we perceive as Self and in our classification and appreciation of everything which we classify as being not a part of I-ness, from the majority of our body experiences to the structure of the universe as seen by mythology and by science. All human perception is egocentric however far its speculative range may extend, and the "microcosm" intuition of some older mysticisms is to this extent perfectly valid and to be reckoned with.

It is difficult but possible to guess intelligently at the actual *processes* involved in I-ness: the problem here is not how a sensorium "perceives" but why it objectifies itself, and how. Memory seems to be at some point involved, in that it is empathically difficult to conceive amnesic I-ness, though the existence of even a short memory-span, rather than a fund of experience, seems, empathically again, to be sufficient. One possible model for a system by which a sensorium would perceive itself as an objectivized being is through the introduction of a delay network. If the encoding process for memory is slower than the registration by non-memory functions of real-time events, and if this delay is brief, the memory-encoded image might be scanned on a par with real-time input and thus objectivized: a simultaneous or delayless selfawareness, by feeding straight back a self-scan of the perceiving process would not do, for it would presumably be inherently unstable.

Homuncularity may in fact be a *déjà-vu* effect—it has a certain aura-like quality. As such it might be accessible to playback interference, as is speech.

In particular, if the time-constants of "total" (gestalt-type, nondiscursive) perception and of logical–linguistic perception are different, whether or not these reside in opposite hemispheres, and if the difference is large in man owing to his verbal capacity, there may be a delay between the two, so that one (presumably the slower, verbal component) objectivizes the other. There is at some point in I-ness a perception which is nearly but not quite a real-time perception, and which determines our intuition of the directionality of time, since the delay is asymmetric and the system cannot be "run backwards."

On this hypothesis, there would be a point in phylogeny where the delay due to an increased logic system would be sufficient to produce objectivization as a significant experience. There would also, since the logical mode in humans both develops and is learned, be a point in childhood where it appeared, as it does, and this appearance would be gradual or partial, as it is. I-ness could be turned off, on the same model, by blocking or suspending the analytic mode from comparison with the analogic—which is what many ecstatic techniques involve. Sensory deprivation would upset it by withdrawal of input—enteroceptive inputs seem to feed directly into the alogical side of the "bridge," the logical side being directed chiefly to sorting input from the outside world. Some inkling of a connection between normal I-ness and a delay element can be had if we watch ourselves in a "delaying mirror" (closed-circuit TV with a 0.5 sec. delay)—the ghost of a second identity sometimes appears under these circumstances. This is quite possibly what we are doing all the time. The hypothesis appears testable and important, not least for its comment on Spinoza's suggestion that the sensation of "willing" an action follows, rather than precedes the inception (whatever that is) of the action in real-time. It may be wrong, but there exists a probability that something like it, in terms of systems theory, is right, and that what we perceive is a delay-generated echo, the objective homunculus. It may not be fortuitous that samādhi means not only monistic ecstasy but equalization—the removal of a delay from one limb of a double system.

Recapitulating the model (fig. 1), assume that exteroceptive input is split between two analyzers, one "intuitive," gestalt and nonverbal, which is both the more primitive and the faster, and one logical–verbal as well as pattern-detecting, which is measurably the slower. Assume also that most enteroception, plus other total-experience inputs, goes chiefly or wholly into channel 1, and that part of the printout of this channel is the "body image," with one or many feedback loops to the body itself. "Perception" is the sum of many outputs to various brain functions—channel 1 encodes these as gestalt and has a "hot line" output into affect: channel 2 has a logical–verbal output which is monitored by channel 1, both as to content and as to match completion and pattern detection: many or all of the pattern-comparison circuits available to channel 2 are drawn from channel 1's body-image circuitry. In such a system, by reason of the delay in one arm of the bridge, the intuitive system objectifies the activity of the logical system (in the Upaniṣadic term, it sees seeing, but *is* the seer of seeing).

Reward mechanisms can be added to such a model. Alogical perception and the fusion of I with channel 1 activity is by report reinforced, or "beatific"—presumably therefore reward results from the (normally unusual) unmodified operation of channel 1. It also results from the situation where a gestalt or pattern intuition generated in channel 1 fits verificatorily with the logic conclusions of channel 2—channel 1's circuitry must accordingly be feeding "intuitive" patterns to channel 2 and monitoring fit. Rewarded physiologic states such as orgasm may, apart from sneeze-type reflex completion, be rewarded to the extent that they turn off logical input from channel 2 to channel 1. For unopposed channel 1 activity to be "blissful," rather than anxiety-producing as in confusional states, channel 2 logic must be actively turned off, spontaneously or by some maneuver. "Bliss" is a thalamic-sounding term, suggesting that channel 1 is as befits the senior system plugged into the thalamus generally as well as by way of the "wiring" of the body image. Rage, incidentally, which is another thalamic mode, does not appear to figure in any yogic accounts of *nirvīkalpa* experiences, even as a hazard or bad trip—the only ethnologic ecstatics who cultivated it were the Berserkers, and they probably do not belong in the model.

The learning store of each channel is available to the other; channel 1 has no circuitry to use "bits" encoded logically by channel 2, but can use abstracted patterns—channel 2 has access to channel 1's pattern store, but since for channel 2 pattern represents the *result* of logical sorting, these patterns carry a conviction of "fit." I-ness accordingly disappears as an objective "thing"—the channel 2 system is engaged in analysis, and one of its perceptions is the activity of the pattern-detecting I of channel 1, which it reads as not-self and objectifies on a par with the body image—a body image cerebral. Or the asynchrony may operate the other way around—the faster channel may observe the operation of the slower, rather than the slower objectify the output of the faster.

I have put this hypothesis at some length because it may be in principle verifiable, and because, as I have said, though it is probably wrong, it lies in the right universe of discourse and something like it is probably right. We may hold it in mind in discussing a particular group of phenomena intimately associated with I-ness which make up the main topic of this study.

It is obvious that if two continuously operating systems differ in time constant, something has to be done to get their act together: if not, mentation would have to resemble Tristram Shandy's diary, where it took a year to write up each day's events. It is not very easy in electromechanical circuitry to slow down a continuous display other than by pulsing it and storing the resulting "bits" for reinjection: how exactly a neurochemical system would address the same problem we do not know, because we have only rudimentary ideas about the nature of brain processing. These, however, are continually becoming accessible to direct experiment. If the faster, gestalt system has to be slowed, it is most likely to be done by the creation of an ongoing display which is then periodically sampled, at the rate of scan appropriate to the processing capacity of whatever is scanning it. The analogy would be to a television camera in a planetary lander

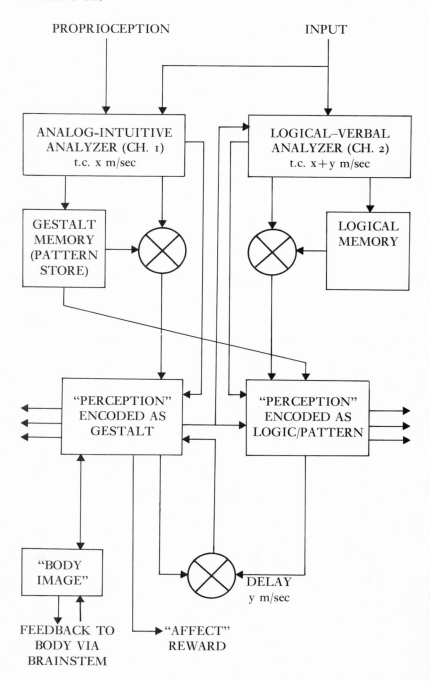

Fig. 1: *A system-theory model of objective identity.*

where only one frame in, say, ten is encoded for transmission back to earth.

Karl Pribram at Stanford has recently suggested that the brain functions not like a computer but like a hologram. A hologram is a photorecord of the interference-fringes produced by wave-fronts reflected at a given wavelength from an array. When viewed in ordinary light it appears as a blur, but when scanned with the coherent beam of a laser, solid objects appear, and can be made to rotate or to move relative to each other by tilting the hologram. Another property of a hologram is that if it is cut up and a small portion is scanned, the whole scene appears, though at a decreasing level of definition—in other words, all parts of the hologram contain all of the information contained in the whole.

On this model, what we normally experience could be the scanned state of the interference-pattern generated in the brain by sensory inputs and by its own activity. In an oceanic or "I-less" mode of perception, the scan could be shut off, and what is intuited would then be the interference-pattern itself. Conventional attempts to represent the oceanic vision as "music of the spheres," a many-petalled lotus, or a receding structure of superimposed triangles, bear some resemblance to, or analogy with, interference patterns, and all such subjective records stress the continuation and heightening of perception, but with the sense of external viewpoint suppressed.

Our only contact with a "real" world is by way of the sensory inputs we receive from it, and the conceptual and classifying processes which go on in the brain. If both of these are expressed in some form of interference-pattern, oceanic states may represent a trick by which this pattern is monitored without being interpreted: in this case the processes connected with our sense of the objective would be of a piece with the rest of the hologram, and the positional "I" would in fact be seen as containing the information of the whole, like any other subdivided hologram. Switch on the scan again and separate objects and concepts would once more be seen as separate.

All of this speculation was initially long on creative theory and very short on experimental fact—before we commit ourselves to a "holographic model" for the brain, there are some awkward questions to ask, not least the nature of the waves of electrical activity which produce the hypothetical interference-pattern: presumably they represent the sum-and-difference of phase relations between the activity of different neurones. Since it is now possible to record brain activity, not as waves, but as a power-spectrum which can be scanned like a hologram, using the circuitry developed for side-looking radar, Pribram's model should be investigable.

This is now proving to be the case. Pribram cites a whole range of neuropsychological studies on image formation to support the active role played by brain mechanisms in putting together "wholes" out of sensory inputs by a combination of computational and optical-type information processes. The momentary states set up in the course of this processing activity closely resemble those of image-constructing devices—in other words they are holographic. The same applies to memory: rules are stored as in a computer, but images are retrieved from a holographic "deep structure." Pribram's own work has shown that the anatomic localization of motor functions in the cortex functions as an "array" on which environmental invariances are displayed. One interesting confirmation of this comes from the discrepancy between two experiments in which kittens were raised in a striped environment. In one, conducted by Blakemore in 1974, the stripes were painted on the walls of the cylinder in which the animals were raised—these kittens were thereafter unable to follow the movement of a bar traveling at right angles to the direction of the stripes. Hirsch and Spinelli, in Pribram's laboratory, raised kittens in striped goggles, and found no change in their behavior as a result. It follows from this that to affect behavior the constant input had to remain invariant across transformations produced by head and eye movements—which is what one would expect of a holographic rather than a "perceptual" mode of processing.

Another explorable possibility is that self-monitoring "identity" involves not time-lag as such but some aspect of phase difference. The idea of objective reality as representing interference pattern, most recently embodied in Karl Pribram's holographic model, is in fact an extremely ancient one. The interesting feature of its antiquity is that until holography rendered it mathematical, this model has always been intuitive, associated with "mysticism," and based on some experiential feature of oceanic experience. From the subjective descriptions of inclusiveness, merging, universality and so on (and attempts to depict these in visualizations such as the "thousand-petalled lotus," the śri yantra, and a wide range of neo-Pythagorean formulae involving "vibrations") it does appear that there are two potential states of perception which are analogous in narration to the perception of a scanned and an unscanned hologram, Pribram's "lensless vision." In the second mode, corresponding to the unscanned power spectrum, the I is suppressed or seen as included in the holographic whole, with the corollary that since all parts of a hologram contain its total pattern at a lower level of definition, the residual I-experience contains "reality" in microcosm. Holographic models are, of course, open to mathematical and experimental examination, both in physics and in neurology. The interest will be to see whether the normal/"lensless" antithesis in oceanic experience is mere analogy, a result of the structure of brain information-handling, an intuition of the potential structure of matter, or both. It does however look possible that advances in conceptual physics are going to involve increasing exploration of neurology, and the structure, not of the observed, but of the theorizing observer—in this area, study of the difference between "normal" and oceanic perception has real heuristic interest quite apart from the physiology of identity.

Pythagoras long since stressed the relation of aesthesis to the recognition of frequency-patterns, and went on to talk about the "music of the spheres." Natural objects often appear to us aesthetic, a point which has sometimes exercised artists and led them to imitate nature: a part of this appeal is very often, it seems, located in the fact that they exhibit regularity and are the result of process—a tree and a geological landscape combine coherent structure and a component related to time: at a given moment they represent, as it were, frames in an arrested film. The element of aesthesis, if we introspect it, does here involve the nondiscursive perception of complex interaction, history, and futurity (we can, of course, with a good deal of labor, spell out the history of the tree in terms of botanical ontogeny, or the landscape in terms of the deposition and attrition of layers, their folding and their angle of lay). The aesthetic, however, when it refers to natural objects not made to communicate a particular sensation, does appear to have something to do with ease of nondiscursive perception—not the analysis of process and pattern, but their recognition, by way of their consonance with our manner of handling them cerebrally. A physical theory is also aesthetic if it "chimes"—if for example it observes symmetry, or models out in a circular pattern, corresponding to a sine-wave. Such preferences have taken second place in science-of-science speculation to the identification of ideological and cultural influences on model-formation. What we have not examined is the extent to which the objective structures which we actually perceive are being modeled by a selection based on the processes involved in perceiving them. Pribram's holographic model brings back the Pythagorean interest in phase and frequency with considerable force—sufficient to make us look for experimental confirmation or an alternative.

Is the "hologram," if it exists, in the brain, in the observed structure of matter generally, or both?

If the human brain itself functions on a holographic model, it is not over-surprising if in certain conditions this model can be itself intuitively perceived and projected on "objective" reality. If "objective reality" itself is holographic, there is no special reason why we should perceive this state of affairs intuitively in some unusual set of neuropsychological conditions. There remains the possibility that both the brain and "objective reality" exhibit holographic properties, either homologous or analogous, so that in intuitively monitoring the structure of brain function we are looking at one model of a generalizable phenomenon, but this would only be analogous to the consonance between the human predilection for circular and orbital systems and our ready detection of circular and orbital models in observed "reality." Structure in "reality" is so much the interpretative projection of the way our brains work that we do not need to go beyond the perception of how we perceive in order to hypothecate intuitions of microcosm and macrocosm as valid. Whether the brain has indeed holographic properties ought to be investigable—even if it has not, or does not work like that, it might still perceive intuitively the structure of such a model, just as it has been able to appreciate its possibility mathematically. Certainly, however, in regard to many phenomena, notably time, it seems likely that future advances in physics may be advances in neurophysiology, and that the making of models for the "objective universe" will increasingly depend on examination of the system to which it appears objective.

In fact, a model for subatomic particle physics in which particles are seen not as structures but as events or loci, corresponding to the nodes of an interference pattern, seems to follow from the work of Chew and the Lawrence Berkeley laboratory on S-matrix theory[18] to explain the paradoxical character of quarks. It would be risky to suggest that the human brain, even though it is the reference instrument for our investigation of matter and wrote the ground-rules for the questions we ask, defining which answers to them appear paradoxical, is adapted to intuit a cosmology based on loci rather than things. If it did, we should presumably have started with this sort of model, rather than hypothecated it through higher mathematics. On the other hand, the implicit assumption that matter consists of "things," and that subatomic particles are "things," is a viewpoint artefact. Most of the dissenting phenomenologies, as Capra's book title *The Tao of Physics* suggests, in which objects are treated as events within a ground or field depending on interaction of its parts, come from cultures which had some systematic interest in oceanic and nonhomuncular experiences. We do not need any softheaded generalization about the brain-as-microcosm, accordingly: the brain-as-perceiving-system model, which reverses the attribution, will do nicely, and is far more in line with critical analysis. Our brain does not have to be universe-shaped, because our projected universe is bound to be brain-shaped; any cultivation of nonhomuncular perception facilitates the hypothecation of a thing-less or holistic universe, and such a model might prove as rewarding as the concept of particles. If time is also a viewpoint artefact, which may well prove to be the case, the structure of the perceiving system will have to be considered at least as seriously in physics as the structure of observed events when they appear to that system. The roughly simultaneous appearance of holograms, holographic models in neurology, and holographic models in physics has the same logic as the simultaneous development of mechanics, of machines, and of the Newtonian universe—if it had not happened we would have had to invent it. For this reason it is a perfectly serious comment that physical discoveries may be made in the future by persons who have some experience of oceanic perception. We may see it introduced into mathematical courses, rather as marine biologists now acquire the skill of skin-diving as a matter of course. It would be interesting, moreover, to apply the formalism of Chew's model not only to particles but also, at a quite different level of organization, to the maintenance of species by canalization. A species, itself a formalism, has an abstract identity, speciation proceeding not gradually, as older theory assumed, but by something more like quantum jumps, intermediate states being "prohibited" by instability. Although this model ignores the flow-sheet pattern usually assumed in evolution, its mathematics might prove extremely instructive to evolutionary genetics. We may be about to enter a general epoch of field theory models where topology replaces process. It is to less precise models of this kind that much oriental philosophy is attuned.

Since the brain and its chemistry consist of matter, we are still left with the problem of how "matter thinks itself," but this is actually no different between the Democritean and the non-Democritean models: it involves a level of organization at which, as in the elephant story, the two models do not differ practically. It would appear that because the brain is a physical structure, not all physical structures can be wholly virtual, on simple Cartesian grounds, but the non-Democritean model is if anything slightly less prone to take refuge in a separate, "psychic," entity in any sense more absolute than as a model in systems theory—certainly not in portentous notions that "all is Mind" or that "matter is thought," which totally confuse structure with system. Any naive idea that everything, including our own nervous system, exists wholly in the imagination suffers the fate common to objects which fly in ever-decreasing circles. The best formulation is that the sensation of abstracted "I" is an active handicap to philosophers in trying to reach a more appropriate systems model, because it introduces a loop into ratiocination which is inherently tautologous: in other words, we or they are asking a non-question in the wrong way. Whether the progress of, say, Kant, or Fichte, round and round this particular loop could be arrested by an application of systems theory and an analysis of I-ness as observerhood is beyond the scope of this discussion.

III.2
Mathematics and identity

Computers, both digital and analog, have been and will increasingly be employed to duplicate processes or tasks undertaken by the human brain. It is easy to move from this—which is in fact a convenience— to the assumption that the analytic processes in actual brains are linear and mathematical. What is more probably true is that mathematics is an adventitious capacity of brains, developed by an inherent capacity for self-experimentation—brains can, empirically, solve equations or categorize sets, but the ability or knack of so doing is a discovered social behavior subject to cultural transmission: there is no evidence that brains function naturally by solving equations or categorizing sets, or that mathematics is an introspection of this process made conscious—any more than that paper doilies have among their functions the capacity to be played on pianolas.

This view is supported by the fact that mathematical analysis is often intuitively opposed to empirical (or brain-type) analysis, and that for purely arithmetic tasks mechanical systems are often superior. The difference seems to lie in the fact that brain-type analysis probably proceeds by rapid comparison of pattern and simultaneous comparison of sub-patterns, with the store of comparison materials derived partly from learning and partly from structure, so that some patterns are, from infancy, preferentially treated: an activation of such preferential treatment by hormones can be observed in animals. This is, in essence, an analog system, but it does not exactly resemble any factitious analog computer, being in general slower but more versatile. The same system, clearly, is capable of mathematics (or we should have none)—Stonehenge is capable of use to predict eclipses, but it may or may not have been so used. If we were Martians familiar only with jet engines we might assume that birds fly by expelling hot gas from their fundament.

The interest of this is that the mathematical approach, which commences by abstraction of the simplified case and increases its dimensions stepwise, appears for its inception to require the experience of identity, it being axiomatic that mathematics requires a mathematician capable of abstracting, i.e. of isolating a particular system, experiencing it as external to I-ness, and conducting operations on it. Accordingly human brain-based mathematics, which look initially like the view of the not-I most invulnerable to subjective distortion, actually require one highly subjective experience (homuncularity) to set the abstractive process in train.

Moreover although mathematical relations can be nondiscursively experienced, by people who already know them discursively, during states, such as those induced by LSD-25, in which I-ness is turned off or altered, the only really intuitive part of the brain's large mathematical potential may well be the starting point—that because there is a mathematician, abstraction as a first step is possible. One might infer, first, that logical–mathematical computer systems, however complex, would not acquire I-ness, because they have it already in the I-ness of those who programmed them to proceed as if an I were calculating, and that I is external to the computing system: and second, that a system which neither itself contained anything analogous to homuncularity, nor had the benefit of a programmer's homunculus, could not perform mathematics, though it could recognize pattern. Further, it might be that an educable system, basically analog, might develop homuncularity, or an equivalent point of view, at the moment when it found that mathematical abstraction was necessary to complete the comparison upon which it had embarked—that would be the time, no doubt, to look out for a "thinking" or humanoid computer.

It is interesting to speculate what would be the form of an observerless mathematics—presumably it would concern matrices rather than functions and specify association between quantities in a nonoperational or simultaneous form. The normal equational pattern, although it is not dealing with any time-based sequence such as causality, is actually modeled on one by the process of presentation in logical steps, as if, when a relationship is put in the form

$$a + b = c \dots\dots\dots\dots\dots\dots\dots\dots\dots\dots\dots\dots\dots\dots\dots\dots\dots\dots\dots\dots\dots$$

the process of adding a to b *caused* the existence of c: not because this is implied, but because it is the most convenient way of printing-in to a time-based, or conventional, human logic system. The equation does not in fact mean "first there were a and b, and their combination produced c," or "a pre-existing c can be split into a and b," but the convention is so natural that we overlook the apparent vector component in the formalism, exactly as we overlook the homuncularity and temporality of the mathematician. Now and again the vector is explicit (usually when diagram replaces algebra; Feynman diagrams are an example) but even in algebra the illusion of sequence influences the encoding process. With very complex problems, e.g. in topology, this actually matters—in fact the advantage of surfaces as models is that they can make simultaneities and remote interdependences visualizable. Einstein is said to have wondered as a boy what would be our experience of light if one could ride a light-wave like a surfer. It is of more than perverse interest to wonder what mathematics would print-in most easily to the mind during an "oceanic" experience. It would have to be an algebra which could not be typed sequentially onto a moving tape.

There are several rather obvious constraints on similarity between neural and electronic computing systems—one is that the neural mode is too slow to proceed usefully by exhaustive enumeration: in fact, it evolved to meet the adaptive value of being able to short-circuit enumerative–stochastic ways of handling situations which biological systems perform slowly. If organisms had been able to add an electromechanical mode, their brain structure might well have pursued a different direction, based on speed of computation: as it was, they were stuck with computational velocities determined by neural, not electronic, hardware, and evolved strategies of successive approximation and total pattern recognition—which, given the system, are the only really feasible ways of boosting response speed and handling capacity. By the time of man, we have a brain where the capacity for recognition, comparison, and abstract handling of pattern, similarity, analogy, homology, and their intraspecific communication as language is superb, but the velocity of specific calculation is low, and requires extra-cerebral crutches at the very lowest level: skilled mathematicians can proceed without a sheet of paper or a blackboard, as some people can play chess in their heads, but it is an effort, and no more the optimal mode of the system than it is for a dog to ride a bicycle.

If our guess is right, it was the stimulus of language and the requirement for social communication which caused the installation of additional circuitry—the ability to objectify (so that there is an I which does the talking, observing, communicating) may have been an uncovenanted result of the real-time slowness of the system, introducing an asynchrony of which evolution promptly took advantage, so that abstraction became possible. The idea identity = language is not new, but such a model suggests how it came about: it is not so much that one becomes an I by talking—rather that in order to talk, one acquires a sense of I. Washoe, the Ameslan-talking chimp, used deaf-and-dumb language to express awareness of identity, even when alone.

The importance of mathematics and of language is that both represent the discursive reduction of patterns, states and relationships which we initially perceive gestalt-wise as wholes. Pythagoras perceived the homology between pitch and wave-motion, but it took several centuries to make the structure of the homology discursively communicable with precision. The same homology could at almost any time have been rendered communicable as poetry or myth, which would have conveyed the same information, but not in a form which exhibits the structure of the homology.

Humans appear normally to perceive structure and relationship first in the gestalt mode, which we have called channel 1, and then by analysis in the discursive mode, which represents the partial reduction of pattern-comparison to its component parts. We have suggested that it is a component of this double process, depending on difference in time constants, which creates the subjective experience of "identity." Any philosophical problem of ontology therefore resolves itself into an analysis of how exteroceptive inputs are treated in the human brain, and how far, since there is "an Outside spread within, and an Outside spread without," consistency of phenomena is determined, and their apparent pattern ordered, by selection and categorization in the observing system. It is a convention that we actually recognize pattern in the discursive terms in which we describe it—in fact, the initial computer-like patterning of our perception is analog, and the repertoire of comparison patterns has been evolved not only to scan "external reality" but also to pattern various internal and possibly also social activities. Categorization and the division of phenomena into classes distinct from internal and uncategorized response is a secondary formation, connected with the capacity to order them for bit-wise communication—our initial perception probably resembles that of oceanic experience in which "reality" is neither distinguished from a personalized observer, nor from somatic experience, nor categorically expressed, but rather incorporated. The result is like the perception of the chessplayer, described by Davy,[19] who saw the game not in terms of successive serial moves but as gestalt—if a piece were surreptitiously removed, the pattern became "meaningless." This player perceived chess oceanically—he did not analyze the game: in an intelligible sense he "was," or incorporated, it. There is a probability that most good chessplayers proceed in the same way, but interpret the game to their abstracted selves by the same process which they would use to describe it to a third party—they serialize it as a sequence of moves depending on the *logical* responses of an objectified I who is the player—precisely as we communicate mathematical structure as a sequence of operations attributed to an objectified mathematician. In the case of chess the degrees of freedom are limited by the rules of the game. In the case of our general perceptions, they are almost certainly limited by the rules of our pattern-recognizing equipment.

Now discursive–linear exposition, like chess, is a conventional or culturally-transmitted mode of proceeding. As a comment on ontology and the nature of the "real" it is a philosophic rather than a religious exercise. At the same time it represents a sophistication of the exercise undertaken less discursively by every primitive who addresses, or is addressed by, a That which he regards as not-Self, and, as we shall see, the linear mode conventional to our culture itself partakes of the character of a religion.

It may, indeed, be of supreme importance to the vast and adaptive human capacity for analysis that there is a department of the

brain which walks, as it were, a step behind nondiscursive perception, monitoring its performance, reclassifying its content, and
functioning precisely as the "seer of seeing"—an abstractive
override which, with its appearance in phylogeny as in ontogeny,
constitutes man as a discursive and abstracting animal.

IV.1
Religion and the experience of "I"

I have discussed I-ness at some length here, because Religion appears to me to be an offshoot or consequence of the homuncular experience, and of its common modifications.

I am taking religion to mean initially a range of behaviors, from the simple and personal to the highly-organized and institutional, by which humans deal with their impression that "the universe addresses us," and by which they attempt to structure relationship and dialog with the not-human (animals, rocks, spirits, deities) whose inherent "personality" they infer, and with not-persons (objects, the universe in more sophisticated orders, the dead—who were persons and are so no longer). It represents accordingly a strong human tendency to project human-like responses into the not-human so that it may be conversed with: these responses are more pretended, hoped for or feared than actually believed, with one exception to which I will come presently—often dialog as between humans is a convenient shorthand, like the inferring of an Evolutionary Demon: many religious behaviors approximate to the biological rubric of play. The aborigine does indeed relate not only practically, but also with emotional involvement to landscape, animals, and weather; children, until adultified, do the same. It involves no categorical confusion to treat things as people—we see the value of the shorthand in modern ecology. It is not far from this shorthand to a genuine αἰδώς or respect for the rights, susceptibilities and rightness of things and the unhuman, which can turn further into fear of the powers and sanctions of the unhuman. Religion differs from sorcery, I think, as automation differs from mechanization—religion implies dialog with, and a kind of cooperation with, the unself and the unhuman; sorcery aims at its manipulation as a source of personal power. The lineal descendant of sorcery is interventionist science—the more ethical and structure-orientated science of the present time is now rapidly developing traits in common with primitive religion.

Because religion is a human behavior it can be said to have a biology. One part of that biology appears already in the human tendency to personalize non-human contacts (this does not have to be genetically built-in to be a substrate for biopsychological investigation). Applying Pangloss' Theorem, one could argue that religious

behaviors are or were probably adaptive. If religious behaviors, or
the timber from which they are made, are an adaptation of man, then
the manifestation of them which would most represent adaptation
"on the hoof" would be that which characterized human life styles
over the first 95 percent, not the most recent 5 percent, of *sapiens*
history. We have only inferential access to this, no Early Men being
available for questioning, but it seems fair to infer that the society
which they had, and the style of their living, were not widely different
from those of Australian Aborigines or Kalahari Bushmen. For both
these peoples, dialog with "nature," though distinguished from
dialog with other persons by being set in a distinct "dream time,"
is an important integrator of their whole self-view in relation to the
world and to activity.

IV.2
Schizophrenics and shamans

More important than the tendency to treat things as people if we are
looking for a specific thing which is both human and unique, is the
one case where, on addressing the universe, we actually get an
answer—or where the nonhuman may suddenly of itself appear to
address us, often to our great alarm. This is the shamanic experience,
the human susceptibility to altered states of consciousness, ranging
from dreams, which we all have, to compelling waking sensations of
otherness, address from without, and oceanic experiences (the
feeling of a total one-ness between all of the surrounding not-Self
and the Self of the observer).

Oceanic experiences characterize mystics: hallucinatory or
dissociative experiences characterize shamans. These represent
different modes, though some of their religious consequences
overlap. In particular shamanism generates affect but not, as a rule,
epistemology. Oceanic and shamanic experiences are in desuetude in
our own culture; the Church views visionary and thaumaturgic saints
like Father Pio with a rather jaundiced eye, the individual who has a
shamanic experience makes no use of it (though, like a shaman, he
may be profoundly altered by it, he gets no social support) and will go
to the doctor if it persists; in fact, the problem for many epileptics
with temporal lobe symptoms, some migraine patients, and, occasionally, the schizophrenic, whose biochemistry sets him apart from
the posture of all those around him, is to stop the attacks of altered
consciousness or, in the case of the schizophrenic, to get back out of

dream time into real-time perception. Few, if any, of those whom the gods or the ancestors now visit spontaneously appreciate the experience or are tempted to shamanize further in order to repeat it. The advent of psychedelic drugs profoundly altered this, and a whole generation deliberately explored this method of shamanizing at a cheap rate. Primitives who have had access to psychedelics have used them in the same way, though with a more structured background to support them—they are, as it were, a phone line to the not-Self enabling us to see the inner colors of rocks, the spirits in trees, and occasionally, if we are susceptible, the Unity of All Things, without the use of exhausting and unreliable techniques such as fasting, whirling, overbreathing, dancing to exhaustion, or lying tied up in a dark igloo while relays of assistants drum in one's ears.

The point here is that, as we have seen, these experiences occur spontaneously in some people, and can be evoked by art in many. They are tangible reinforcements of the existing human impression that the nonhuman is probably in its own way personal; and, that some of its components internal to ourselves are so close to the I as to be Selves also: they can produce blinding conviction, even in sophisticated and blasé moderns; they totally alter the "set" of some individuals who undergo them.

There are unspontaneous shamans—once the shaman has office and prestige, people will shamanize to acquire it. In modern shamanistic cultures, quite a few practitioners are at least as much showmen as shamans. The spontaneous shaman, however, is often "changed" by his experience to become desocialized, eccentric, privileged, or (literally) inspired. In the extreme stability and unenterprise of a tribal setting, he can become the human emissary of the Yoruba Trickster God, without whom nothing would happen because nothing would change.[20] It could be that in a primitive culture some schizophrenics are adaptive for the society if not for themselves—in fact, the original in most such societies who wants to overrule custom can best do it by having a vision, proclaiming himself possessed, or taking a shamanic *sādhana* such as cross-dressing or acting backwards—as the old Quakers would have said, "for a sign." The shaman, moreover, because he can move freely between human and nonhuman, is the interface man—he can help us manage disease or disaster, deal with nonpeople such as spirits, and personify the integration of self and environment. He can overrule dominance structures by outclassing noninspired magnates.

It could be argued that if spontaneous shamanic experiences, which are often associated with what we now know as pathology, had not been useful to man they would not have stayed in the repertoire—this, like all appeals to indirect selection, is biologically dubious. What does appear important for man, though until lately in disuse, is the capacity for altered-consciousness experiences—they very possibly have functions. I have written elsewhere about the neurological trick or final common path by which oceanic, "astral" and revelatory experiences probably depend, and on the sense of revelation which accompanies them.[21] They are the product of the brain, not the gods and ancestors, but it is only our disabling religious literalism which devalues them on this count—how else, except with our nervous system, can we have such sensations? We are the computer which we are using: the yogic skill of using manipulation of the body image to manipulate the body is more recent and, in its way, less fundamental, than the use of altered states of consciousness to interface the self with other of our selves and with the Other, a necessity of the localized identity-sense which characterizes man and has played so large a part in his discursive creation of a world picture. The localized, linear, scientific man of the urban societies, who tends not to treat things as people, but people as things (because he passes more of them ungreeted in a single day than an Aborigine sees in a lifetime), and who normates experience and environment as seen by a point source sitting in the head and looking forwards, like a car driver, finds the experiences "God addresses me," or "I am That" far more alien than does a Bushman or an Eskimo (many shamanic societies are small, and the interactions of the individual with people few: in such a setting, rocks are more nearly people than in Los Angeles). A rabbit, with 360° vision, experiencing himself as a sense-of-position only would have a different mysticism if rabbits were mystical. This is not a facetious comment. When Stone Age Man wished to numinize an object, he drew a face on it.[22]

Religion is a human and characteristic behavior. It has become elaborate; it has been systematized, hierarchized, developed and literalized as does any other basic human matrix of experiencing once fed into the machinery of the restless human social mind. But I think our definitions, at least in regard to its biology, should be directed to the essential experiences, rather than what has been built on them. Among these is the projection of humanness on the nonhuman (it is hard for a modern adult not to see a steam locomotive as a person; a Californian airline paints a grin on its aircraft to reduce their threatening augustness). They reflect the capacity for altered and oceanic experiences, produced or coming upon us unawares, which seems to chime with the conviction that the nonhuman possesses a face: so that we explore the interface between human and not-human, employ ritual to control it, and invoke the help of those who seem adept in crossing it, whether by endowment or through *tapas* and sādhana. This seems to me part of the "biology" of religion.

At some point the personalization of things involves us further with ethics. As social animals we are programmed to be aware, as are dogs, of the opinion and reaction of other humans. If things, the weather, the rocks, and kangaroos have attributes, however larval, of humanness, we must take account of their feelings. Finally, we may project dominance out of the group altogether and attribute to them, or to a god or gods, an overriding vote in how we should act, such as our parents had in childhood, who now, as ancestors, are among the august departed. The powers of the nonhuman are, to the primitive, truly overriding—one dry season can wipe out the tribe—and if the nonhuman is addressable, it is also to be reverenced. These, then, are phenomena we should class as basically religious, and part of the evolved pattern of man. Whether we call them adaptive, like our social–ethical behaviors, or simply serendipitous is beside the point; but they are very characteristic of humanness. If we found tools and remains which might be human or prehuman, it would settle the matter in favor of humanness if we found evidence, not of language or fire, which are pre-*sapiens*, but of art, or of religious, interfacing behavior: burial, worship, circumcision, ritual. These things would be the unequivocal markers of humanness: they express a self-regarding sense of personal identity, since to recognize a That one must first distinguish an I, and then hypothecate its relation to the not-I which stands over against it. The chimpanzee, instructed in sign-language by man, does the first, but probably not the second.

The best list of "religious" behaviors is that derived by A. F. C. Wallace:[23]

1. Addressing the supernatural (prayer, exorcism).
2. Music (dancing, singing, chanting, playing instruments).
3. Physiological exercise (physical manipulation of psychological states through drugs, deprivation and mortification).
4. Exhortation (addressing others as representative of divinity).
5. Reciting the code (use of the sacred written and oral literature, which contains statements regarding the pantheon, cosmology, myths and moral injunctions).
6. Simulation (imitating things for purposes of control).
7. Mana (touching things possessed of sacred power; laying on of hands).
8. Taboo (avoiding things to prevent the activation of unwanted power or undesired events).
9. Feasts (sacred meals).
10. Sacrifices (immolation, offerings, fees).
11. Congregation (processions, meetings, convocations).
12. Inspiration (pursuit of revelation, conversion, possession, mystical ecstasy).
13. Symbolism (manufacture and use of symbolic objects).

V.I
The boundaries of religion

Whitehead's much-quoted remark[24] that "Religion is what the individual does with his solitariness" seems to have been widely misunderstood. William James[25] put it better—"Religion therefore shall mean for us the feelings, acts and experiences of individual men in their solitude, so far as they apprehend themselves to stand in relation to whatever they may consider divine." Leaving aside the divine That, the point about solitude is not the privacy of the experience—religions are commonly, though not always, socially reinforced and social in at least part of their content—but the primacy of the I experience, which is as it were the kernel of "solitude," as being separate from That. We should do better to rewrite these definitions in the terms that religion is what the I experiences in setting its boundaries, including the experience of two-way traffic with the nonhuman not-I. It will be seen that this leaves open the presence or absence of a theology, for part of the not-I with which such dialog may be had is the range of brain processes not incorporated into the I-experience, including larval, subsidiary or temporarily segregated parts of the software of our own identity, and, beyond these, external patterns, which may be inanimate but address us by consonance with our own capacities of pattern-detection. As to whether any part of the nonhuman not-I has mindlike properties, we may assign these as objective or projective according to taste and to our definitions of mind.

Scientific literalism, aside from having been genuinely useful to man, is basically a process of self-defense of the objectivized I, reified by Blake as Newton. Our respect for it (and our justified distrust of people like Teilhard de Chardin, who have intuitions and experience *bhakti*, but can't function in the linear discipline as well as in the imaginative where that is appropriate) may make us miss the hardnosed character of Blake's formulations viewed as science. One of these, from *The Marriage of Heaven and Hell*, summarizes the whole epistemology of the I–That–body image complexity, much more briefly than I can in the discursive form: "Man has no Body distinct from his Soul, for that called Body is a portion of the Soul discerned by the Five Senses, the chief inlets of Soul in this Age. Furthermore, Energy is the only life and is from the Body; Reason is the bound or outward circumference of Energy."[26] Leaving aside the meanings we now attach to "soul" and "energy," this puts things in a nutshell. What we call body is a fusion of sensory inputs with body image, both scanned by the I-experience ("soul") which is in turn an energetic or phenomenal activity of body processes. Reason, or linear-scientific thought, is a deliberate bounding of this process, and *pari passu* a limitation of the I itself, which does the research and inference required by science—which is in turn the "religion" of this mode of I-expression. Other religious and imaginative modes alter the bounds. They are not appropriate to linear-type undertakings— on the other hand, one does not wear protective clothing all of the time, only for special purposes. Linearity of thinking is a special-purpose activity for man, highly adaptive where relevant, and disadaptive as Blake insists it to be where exclusive or applied to the inappropriate. That we are becoming able to use the linear (neurology, pharmacology) to gain insight into the allusive and imaginative is the privilege, perhaps, of the age—we badly need both thought and imaginative feeling.

Hindu philosophy is a unique example of the intellectual development of an experience: the entire corpus of the *Upaniṣads* and of later Hindu religious literature depends on the prototypic experience that objective perception is contingent: all the subsequent discourse upon the universal character of Brahman, on the continuity of I with That, and the philosophical and theological development of subsequent schools, is an attempt to render into an ontology and to interpret the conviction carried by exposure to oceanic perception, while the body of yogic, ritual and ascetic practice is aimed to prepare for and induce that experience and render it repeatable at will. This is in sharp contrast to the Judaeo–Christian tradition, in which oceanic experience is a rare and untrustworthy visitation upon a few unorthodox mystics. It is also a reflection of the impressive character, to the seer, of the suspension of the normal mode of perception and of the sense of elation and insight which results from the merging of objective That with subjective I—an experience so impressive that its creation, or re-creation, becomes a life-work and the search for repetition of the experience an addiction. The language of the *Upaniṣads* acquires special interest in view of the model we have suggested, because it implies intuition that somehow the normal process of I-formation and objectivization depends on a duality in viewing. Whether the original source of this experience was pharmacological or not (the Vedic references to *soma* suggest that it may have been), later and modern régimes for producing it have depended on body-image manipulation and meditative techniques of high technical sophistication.

That a vivid perception of the existence of an alternative way of experiencing reality should be philosophically impressive is not surprising. The affective result—usually described as "bliss"—is more interesting and often overlooked. Although the word *ananda* (mystical bliss) figures in the name of every Hindu monk, few modern Hindus who repeat the tradition are much enamored of the *ananda-mimamsa*, or catalog of the degrees of bliss, in the *Brhad-āranyaka Upaniṣad*, which rates the experience of the mystic as being degrees of magnitude higher than that of any other being. Conventional emphasis is more often on the elements of duty, clean living and hard work involved in getting there. The ingredients of the blissful experience appear to be (1) sense of truth or rightness; (2) sense of contentless comprehension; (3) sense of nonseparateness. The last of these may be psychoanalytically the easiest, since it involves "positive expansion" and a reversal of individuation, but the other two seem to be the total activation of the reward-mechanism attached to the human need to comprehend. It is not hard to see why the removal of categorical distinctions should be so esthetically pleasing—it involves the perception of effortless pattern which includes the Self, comprehension in its etymological rather than its intellectual sense, and the suspension of the arduous process of subdividing reality into logically related "bits." The mystic is for the first time seeing the wood rather than the trees.

So selective and explicit a relation of the I-experience to religion-making is unusual. It does, however, give us insight into the blinding conviction which is a feature of religious experience when that experience is compelling and not merely formal. In Hinduism this is explicit and primary, not muffled, incidental or supererogatory.

V.2
Literalism as religion

If religion is the interpretation of the relationship between I and That, then the religion of the dominant civilizations since the end of the eighteenth century has been objectivism—the attempt, that is, to fortify as strongly as possible the boundary between the observer, seen as a kind of point source, and a logically consistent system of external reality. The function of the scientific method is precisely to minimize the role of "structures" due to human modes of perceiving, and to identify structures, and systems of cause and effect, which would be as they are in the absence of a percipient I. The gains which this convention has produced in our manipulative ability *vis-à-vis* matter and energy are evident: the losses, a favorite subject of complaint by seers such as Blake and Novalis whose intuitive perceptions were more complex, are not due to the demoralizing effect of the exercise, but simply to the preoccupation of every age with its own style.

It was necessary to accept the "as-if" implied in scientism if science was to work; it was probably necessary for science to work before the reservations on objectivism could be comfortably admitted through science itself observing them, for once objectivism becomes established as an intellectual and religious style, scientization is sanitization. It has taken particle physics and neurology to combine in demonstrating the intuitive structures concealed in objective "reality," and anthropology to recognize the limitations of a style in which the machine-like analogy applied by the nineteenth century to nature, society, the mind, medicine, and in fact every observable universe of discourse is made to pattern human behaviors and the human self-estimate. In other words, the experimental-objective method has been justified because it has in fact discovered its own limitations—intuitivism will never look the same again because we have learned to be critical about it: the requirement for a more comprehensive philosophy of our perception of structure and of the I–That relationship is not either–or but both–and. We now know that induction is a post-formation—it is the way that science is written up in a paper, not the way in which it happens: what usually occurs is that intuition or imagination comes first, and is then monitored more and more strictly for fit to the "objective." In William Blake's poetical ontology, Urizen the spirit of objective science is an integral part of spiritual wholeness—when he appears as a demon, or tyrant, assisted by Locke and Newton, his familiar spirits, in creating the hell-on-earth characteristic of Faustian literalism and abuse of power, dogma and technology, that is because in so doing he is unsupported by the other three "spiritual senses"—passion, sensuality, and—quintessentially—imagination. When in Blake's eschatology these four human styles or attributes "get their act together," the result is wholeness, and Locke and Newton take their place in clouds of glory along with Chaucer and Milton, whom Blake selects as the mythical heroes of Imagination.

Blake's prediction is in this case absolutely accurate, in that whatever the damage done to man by psychopathic abuse of literalism and technology—which may yet prove irremediable—a return to a proper functional balance between the mythical–analogic and the scientific–linear faculties of intellect, and to the style embodying such a balance, can now come only through comprehension and through empirical experiencing of the ways in which the identity experience can be manipulated. Anything less would be an equally destructive return to an equally pathological antirationalism, which was the last thing that Blake's onslaught on blinkered scientism was intended to bring about.

Not only is objectivism in fact the religion of our culture, but for all its practical advantages it has succeeded in diverting, or contaminating, "religion" in its accepted sense with a linear and historical objectivity alien to the acategorical experience on which it was founded. The significance of the Last Supper and of the Christian sacrament derived from it require no discursive explanation. An Aborigine would accept their purpose without question. Yet throughout the Middle Ages and on into the Renaissance, blood was shed, and our entire understanding of matter and semantics distorted, by the attempt to find some literalistic sense in which bread might be considered to become flesh. The misfortune of historicity has fallen particularly heavily upon Christianity, because it took origin in one specific event, the "truth" of which in a literal sense has always been crucial to its adherents—if Christ be not risen, then are we of all men the most miserable—and the preliteral or experiential view, that He dies every Good Friday and rises every Easter Monday, or that death and resurrection, whether or not they occurred exactly as described in the Gospel narrative on one specific and historical occasion, exist *sub specie aeternitatis*, has been heretical and is still felt as unsettling by believers. At the same time, the Christian religion remains in vigor, not only as a paśu religion of passive assent or political organization, but through the continuous generation of persons whose doctrinal subtlety is minimal, but who believe that "Christ lives in them," or who base their conviction, though not their verbalization, on what is essentially an inner experience of encounter; no amount of irrationality or churchification can dispel the conviction arising from alternative vision, even though the dress which that vision takes was woven by doctrinal preconceptions. Blake was accordingly absolutely right in his insistence that objectivism is the father both of abstractive science (which he saw as evil unless qualified by Imagination, or spiritual sense) and of Nobodaddy, the non-God of non-experience who subsists by rules rather than experimentation—and who, incidentally, has wound up being slain by Science, because the analogic and nonliteral models drawn from introspection, when turned into equivalents of literal history and literal cosmology, have turned out to be simply untrue in the scientific sense: they were competing in the wrong league, and left Christians looking for the literal remains of the Ark, and squabbling over whether Adam and Eve, august and important inhabitants of the Dream Time, were literal persons carrying all the genetic material of all subsequent humans. No Aborigine confuses the mystical Ancestor Serpent Tjurungur with the zoological variety. Rocks are both rocks in common observation, and the bones of Tjurungur in the Dream Time. Our immensely successful use of the linear–objective mode would have been impossible without this transformation to old-fashioned rationalism, and is justified, eventually, in that it is on rationalistic grounds that we now are able, and indeed obliged, to look again at the self-objectivization which made the treatment of That as not-I possible. Nor need we remythologize cosmology or history to do this—Russell defined religion as a passionate belief in nonsense. We can see why literalism has caused the paśu to talk nonsense, and why the empirically religious went on believing in their experiential insights undisturbed by the nonsenses they talked.

V.3
Ontogeny, identity and the philosophy of Śaṅkara

It must be clear from what we have said that ontology is an interface discipline—it exists at the interface between "things" perceived as real and a perceiving and evaluating observer. An interface has two sides. Accordingly, behaviors which operate on the experience of I are at least one half of the equation.

There are, of course, charismatic experiences which are wholly a matter of human interaction—"consciousness raising" of various kinds in the mode of humanistic or existential psychology, which bears a strong resemblance to the experience commonly shared by religious devotees (openness, koinonia, and a heightened sense of one's own identity and that of others). Theologians viewing some of these behaviors tend to identify them as being of the nature of "religion": Indeed, most modern institutional religion gives its adherents far more experience of "we" than of That.

Although "consciousness raising" does not imply at first flush any attempt to address or be addressed by the universe (it is more a matter of getting one's head straight to the point at which one can address or be addressed effectively by other humans) it is, where genuine, profoundly concerned with ego development, in a form which hypostasizes genuineness as a value and heightens the accuracy and warmth of our interaction with others. If we define religious behaviors as human expedients to communicate with, or at least relate to, the not-human, it seems to be a corollary of this that they include attempts to delimit the self, while the treating of things as people goes with a sharper expertise in treating people as people. Our "true identity" is probably best defined, like Brahman, in terms of what it is not, or we are not. If we see "religious" behaviors in man as centered in the experience of Self and of Other, we can see how they become involved in ethics. There are basically two parties to this *dvaita vedānta*, Self and the Other; and the Other includes both others and the not-human. Others impose demands on us and exercise relationships with us which as social beasts we are programmed to reciprocate. Possibly, we surmise on a basis of these experiences, the not-human does so as well. Humanistic psychology puts this in a more interpersonally-centered way than does theistic religion (something nearer "Love is God" than "God is love"); but the Self–Other experience has a similar biology.

This relationship of religion to the identity-experience is in fact the conventional view of much of Hinduism. Śaṅkara[27] puts it explicitly as follows:

> "All mental modifications are objects for the 'I.' It is the knower in all states of cognition, the seer in all altered states of mind, the essence of which is simply the quality of consciousness. But it is through such alterations that the 'I' is discerned, as being central to them and non-different from them. There is in fact no other way of becoming aware of the 'I.' Accordingly, when Brahman is recognized as the inner 'I' of all states of awareness, it is rightly known—that is the substance of insight. Because it is the witness of *all* such altered states we recognize that Brahman shares the identity of the observer, neither more nor less—it is eternal, essential and quintessential 'I,' unparticularized and the same in all beings. 'I'-ness has no distinctive marks—space is space, whether it fills a clay pot or a cave."

All the materials of the religious experience are here in sophisticated guise, but their simpler uses are essentially identical even if less insightful. Śaṅkara is in fact preaching against the dialog of I with That (dvaita) and asserting that I *is* That, a position, as we have seen, which can be taken two ways, according to the interpretation we place on the idea that the That of religions is within us. The simplistic alternatives are neuropsychiatric, that the That is a projection of the I, and the theistic, that the I comprises a spark of self-subsistent That, "man has the infinite within him" (Von Hugel). Śaṅkara inclines to the second, but has too sophisticated a view of the possible effect of inner on the validity of outer cosmology to put it in a naive form.

In fact Śaṅkara's version, which looks exotic to us in its Sanskrit dress, has abundant European counterparts, which would have looked exotic to Śaṅkara by reason of the doctrinal appendages which they attach to the word "God"—when Spinoza defines "body" as a mode which expresses in a certain determinate manner the essence of God, and "thought" as a mode which expresses the nature of God, Śaṅkara would have had no problems in assenting, provided that

Spinoza's God is his I or Brahman. If we by contrast have a problem in our analysis of religion as an attempt to order our identity experience, it is because Śaṅkara's I and Spinoza's God are in this context identifiable with the That with which identity is attempting to construct a dialog. Like Śaṅkara, however, we are bound to wind up either repudiating the antithesis or confused as to the meaningfulness and investigability of the boundaries involved, which is precisely what the advaita philosophy predicts.

From the standpoint of religious behaviors, this whole contrast between "Oriental" and "Western" approaches nicely illustrates the divergence of streams in the matter of rationalizing the human objectified identity-experience—one leans heavily on mystical–fusional experiences ("I am That"), the other objectifies personality and calls: "Is anyone there?" Śaṅkara does not specifically ask how much of the "objective" world is a reflection from, or a transduction through, the I-process, for his tradition is not greatly interested in objective science. Objective science, on the other hand, is liable to run into very awkward confrontations with these repercussions of I-ness which arise from the fact that when we operate with systems, using our minds, there is a genuine non-difference between inner and outer pattern which may or may not be usefully deified, but which affects the sort of objectivity we can reasonably assert for practical uses.

Hardy[13] makes, though in a different context, the observation that the major objectivization involved in theistic religion, namely That or God set over against the objectified I, is at some point involved with the problem-solving mechanism: it is "partly transcendent and felt as the numinous beyond the self, and partly immanent within (the self) . . . it may well be this . . . power which does in fact activate the subconscious solution-providing mechanism in a way which would not otherwise be possible." Solution-providing implies pattern-scanning: "deity" or the numinous in objectified cosmology is perceived in the simplest theogonies as pattern or structure, but what is actually being perceived is resonance between structural pattern in the mind and the eclectic analysis of inputs. This implies a novel reversal of the argument from design, in that what is both inside and outside, immanent and transcendent is pattern. Objectified I-ness is the point of concentration, or scanning, of these consonances, and perhaps because of the incorporation of this experience in the analytic process *pattern itself acquires elements of I-ness* and every problem-solving system is readily personified— not, in normal states of objectivizing consciousness, as not-different from I, but as *an* I which can be treated as wholly objective, wholly subjective, or, as in Hardy's formulation, both by turns or a little of each. The empathic drive behind this may well come from the most adaptive feature of human mind—the fact that the relevant perception of pattern is rewarded, whether it be Kekulé's intuition of the benzene ring, Watson and Crick's of the double helix, or Handel's Hallelujah Chorus, which gave him a vision of God on a great white throne.

In case this sounds unduly rarefied, it is interesting to note one practically important consequence of the homuncular identity experience insofar as it affects physics: Post has suggested, probably correctly[28] that our intuitive attribution of transcendental identity to objects is anthropomorphic, arising from the identity which we attribute to ourselves and to persons. This intuitive attribution is valid for the haeceitas of macroscopic objects, but in particle physics it generates Bolzmann's paradox. Post argues that of Locke's three types of individuality, the physical kind is actively misleading in physics; the biological is doubtful, as it may be being reduced to physical terms, leaving only the type associated with consciousness, which owes its distinctive behavior to memory. I have not here gone into the continuity or noncontinuity of a wholly amnesic ego—my point is simply the cosmological bias imposed by the I-experience in the matter of identity. Śankara would probably also have been exercised by the fact that while we objectivize this-ness in objects such as billiard balls, we tend to neglect its implication of a percipient observer. This is only one instance of the kind of consideration which makes it extremely hard to plump for any naive theology of the nature of a dialog between inner and outer, I and That, or even I and environment. The subtlety of the homuncular illusion is a confusing factor underlying almost every human formulation about "external" events, even where explicit introspection appears to be carefully excluded. This is not a plea for irrationalism, so much as for the application of reason to the character of ratiocination: a conclusion that the Brahman of Śankara's formulation is wholly internal does not therefore exclude some of the cosmological conclusions which a Hindu attaches to his more overtly theistic version.

> "Quid mirum noscere mundum
> Si possunt homines, quibus est et mundus in ipsis
> Exemplumque dei quisquis est in imagine parva?"[29]

> "What wonder if men, who themselves contain the cosmos, and each of whom is the model of deity writ small, can know the wonders of nature?"

Jung[30] quotes this in an essay on the synesthetic use of words by "primitives"—an odd word to choose, since most of his examples come from Sanskrit—but does not extend it to the point Manilius is making—the synesthetic use of Self and our tendency to project what are in fact proprioceptive processes into cosmologies.

V.4
Revelation

There is little point in trampling once more over the old field of the "origins of religion." Clearly these are diverse, according to the religious behavior we are examining—and in any case if we are giving religion a biology we have to start from the range of behaviors we now see. I have tried to define these as behaviors delimiting the I and its attempts at inner dialog with That. On the other hand it is difficult to resist the conclusion that spontaneous I-changing experiences— which include both ecstatic states and, for primitives, dreams—are part of the basis on which interpretative or ritual structures have been erected. In the case of "oceanic" states, the seers experience them, but are in a minority: rituals are devised to make the experience more general, or for use under the influence of the experience (as some films are meant to be viewed when stoned) and later become rituals-for-their-own-sake. It has been suggested[31,32] that the visionary bases of the Veda originated pharmacologically in the Soma cult, and that the rituals enjoined were meant to "go with" the Soma "high"—with the depletion of the supply of Soma, or the movement of the culture away from its sources, ritual became ritual, and a self-subsisting concern: seers, however, recognized that an ingredient was missing, and began to practice the rituals mentally, as coded biofeedback instructions, using a mental (*mānasa*) cup, fire, etcetera, and replacing pharmacology with yoga. Gods in such dispensations, and "idols," which are basically foci for meditation, may, like the thunder god Rudra, be natural forces personified, but they are primarily yantras (implements) for inducing experiences, as masks in innumerable simple cultures are instruments for inducing experiences—a role in which they work on areligious moderns, as any leader of a class on miming with masks will testify.

Obviously not all cult objects are in this sense yantras, but any upon which a potential seer may meditate is a potential yantra—the crucifix is a cardinal example. Not all rituals are derivatives of, or prescriptions for, dissociative ecstasy, but a number which are otherwise unintelligible may have this potential, and may work alarmingly or unexpectedly on those who perform them to fortify rather than reset the boundaries of their culturally prosaic I-experience. Finally, not all religions are or were ecstatic, and the proportion of their adherents who experience altered states of I-ness, like the proportion who are predominantly homosexual, will vary with time and place (the two are curiously analogous, being universal potentials irregularly expressed according to cultural encouragement or discouragement). On the other hand, it is defensible to argue that where the bulk of activity in *a* "religion" is devoted to political, philosophical, social or other ends unrelated to the examination and manipulation of I versus That, then to that extent it is not functioning as a religious behavior, and that a religion totally devoid of the experience of transformed consciousness, a paśu's religion, is a "stickit" religion. Given the human trend to codify, and to turn rituals into folk-ways, a religious "stream" will oscillate between ecstatic, ritualistic, reinterpretative, and neo-mystical periods and individuals, with charismatic (I–Thou) elements thrown in. But basically theology and worship-practices look uncommonly like a Taj Mahal erected over the altered I-states of the shaman and the seer, pharmacological, meditative, or theoleptic: they originate in "revelation," meaning our compelling encounter with parts of our own inner structure seen as not-Self. And "revelation" expresses the fact that there exists a state or states in which experience can become nonhomuncular and nondiscursive, in which the I is stilled, and the focus of perception becomes other or unconventional, so that the I when re-established, or during its quiescence, is "addressed." There are clearly many such states, or one state which is structured as to degree and emphasis, and the content of the address ranges from nil or ineffable to the highly specific (a spoken injunction to build a shrine and deliver a message, as in the case of St Bernadette Soubirous)—seers are not deculturated by what they see or hear. But the physiology of the experience, if we could observe it, is probably simple, and its function either primarily or secondarily adaptive—at least we can entertain the hypothesis that it is adaptive, even if it proves, like double-jointedness, to be an irrelevant capacity, and that what is really adaptive is the human ability to make use of all or any of the possibilities of self-manipulation.

Certainly not all religion, or all behaviors intelligibly religious, are mystical or based on personal revelation. On the other hand, one highly important criterion of a sect is that it coheres less through shared opinion than through shared experience, the consequence of which is to make the world, and the universe of discourse, look different—often dramatically so. Yinger[33], in a prolonged functionalist description of religious behaviors, gives us sects classified as "acceptance sects," "aggressive sects," and "conversionist sects," but not experiential sects (though possibly we should not expect too much from a terminology in which the Salvation Army figures as "Gnostic"). The natural history of sect formation, however, tends (in all but those examples, barely to be called sects, where adherence is a matter of mere opinion) to include a point at which "something clicks" in the mind of the neophyte and identity is differently experienced—a phenomenon of conversion. Arthur Koestler was converted in this way to Marxism by reading, John Bunyan to evangelical conviction by what seemed to him like the voice of God. There certainly are religions which do nothing much to ego-boundaries, but they tend to be tepid, formalistic, paśu religions, which one inherits by birthright like membership of a club. By contrast the various "growth experiences" which offer to seekers a certain amount of explanatory dogma, but quintessentially and in the first place an experience, which they recognize from their own reactions as potentially changing to those who undergo it, are active religions even though secular.

VI.1
Religion and displaced sexuality

Psychoanalytic concepts of religion have relevance to its general biology in that they focus attention on the fact that the self as we experience it, and a variety of behaviors connected with our adoption of standards, real or imaginary external parental figures, and powerful inner convictions belong to infantile experience, father, mother and child being the figures of a family trinity which patterns all these manifestations. Freudian views of religion have tended to see it as an aberration, natural to man but displaceable by insight—Jungian as a paradigm of a number of important mental structures common to humans (which Jung himself was inclined to mysticize rather than to regard as evolved adaptations, but no matter) and to this extent as functional. Sexuality and its repudiation through biologically patterned guilt or avoidance over incest and the Edipal dominance-situation figure chiefly in the Freudian view, which lends itself particularly well to the explanation of our own familiar religious tradition: Freud's own religious background, in Judaism, overtly identified a patriarchal God, and its derivative, Christianity, has been militantly antisexual. It is certainly not wise, however, to generalize these attitudes to human "religious" behaviors as a whole, not all of which are parent-appeasing or ascetic. Sexuality and the intense experiences connected with it, both at the infantile and adult levels, are a common ingredient in the I–That dialog, but Jung, whose field of cultural investigation was wider, is closer to recognizing religion as an adaptive behavior in spite of his disabling unwillingness to look for the biology of the experiences he catalogs.

Ferenczi traces the development of science from magic by way of religion as a progress from the infant illusion of omnipotence (magic) via the childish projection of overwhelming power upon the Other (religion) to a "creative oscillation" between the recognition of our powers and the constraints of reality. This relates religion to the development of our awareness of ego boundaries, but does not make a very good fit with observed human behaviors. Ferenczi knew some "psychics" but no primitive magicians, though Jung and Róheim did. In practical matters, magicians act very like scientists—their powers depend on painstaking discovery of the right maneuvers to control the not-self, and they are profoundly aware of its hazards, which they view much as we do radioactivity.

Religion as self-abasement before a parental God is familiar enough in our tradition. It is in fact post-Christian rather than Judaic in its masochistic form: Abraham and Job had a more humanly parental God who could be argued and bargained with—self-immolation based on the child's surrender of sexuality to an Edipal parent, which we take for granted under cover of unexamined religious stereotypes such as meekness and purity, represents a cultural deviation rather than an identificatory character of "religion," and both Blake and Gnosticism recognize such a god as internal, not transcendent.

Self-annihilation in mystical traditions, identified with eventual mortality and the unreality of the real, and expressed in the profound ikon of the Goddess Kālī, is a little different, for it turns on the attempt to fuse the self with the transcendent That, in experience at least. One trouble is that the versions of Hinduism most popular in the West are rather naturally those which adopt an asceticism in line, superficially at least, with that popular in our own culture of martyred saints and the virtues of unpleasure for its own sake. The concept of "controlling the senses" as askesis—in order the better to listen, as it were—has this additional implication for some but not all sadhus. There is no shortage of sermons in this vein directed to the West—by Hare Krishna or Ramakrishna sadhus, for example: the difference can be seen by comparing the practical asceticism of Ramakrishna himself or of St Francis, with the vulgar anti-sexualism which does duty for it in popular preaching. The equally vigorous orgiastic tradition of other Vaiṣṇava or Śaiva sects is equally misread here as antinomian. Between these extremes, example is the simplest illustration—a less familiar and equally orthodox Vaiṣṇava sermon might run as follows:

"The goswamis devote themselves to controlling the senses, and by *vairāgya* [heroic effort] they succeed in so doing. Yet, by all this hard work, what are they doing? They are focusing attention upon the senses as much as if they were libertines.

"A farmer kept dogs to protect his flock. They were indeed fierce; and, in time, became so many and so importunate that he was afraid of them. Soon, feeding them took up all his time and he had none left for farming. A sadhu who stayed at the farmer's hut said, 'Surely you are the servant of your dogs. This is not good—a man who is the servant of dogs cannot reach perfection.' When he had gone, the farmer said, 'It is true—so long as these animals rule me, I shall never make a living, let alone achieve perfection.'

"What should he do? If he says, 'I will not feed them', he cannot work or think of spiritual matters because of their howling; and they may tear him to pieces. If he ignores the howling and concentrates his mind on Brahman, they will die and he will have no dogs. What he should do is to feed them when hungry; subdue them in his service; keep them to heel; and not let them dominate

87

him either by running his life or by howling because he is starving them. Then, he is a farmer of flocks and not of dogs.

"We should not waste our energies on a great struggle to subdue the senses, but rather feed the dogs so that they do not bark. Do not waste strength in an exhausting struggle to practice austerities.

"Moreover by dealing with the senses in this way, we can employ them, as the farmer does his dogs, to serve us, not in an *āsuran* or *adhīran* [antinomian] way, but as part of the Great Feast. Food is not gluttony but *prasada* [sacrament]; sex is not lechery but a part of the *līlā*. Why else are feasting and lovemaking used as types of the pastimes of the Divine, if they bear no resemblance to what we can experience; or if such things are for us always spiritually hindering? This too is *sādhana*, but not tapas. Those who wallow in abstinences lose the playfulness of the divine pastime, just as those who pursue only pleasures lose its divinity. This is the teaching of the *Chāndogya Upaniṣad*: '*na kāncana pariharet, tad vratam* . . .' 'Do not abstain from woman—that is the teaching.'"

It would be tempting, though mischievous, for a Western scholar to confront puritanical and renaissance Hindu pandits with some of their own canonical texts, rather as Africans confront formalist missionaries with their own Bible. Bhaktivedanta Prabhupada and his Hare Krishna charismatics, who have encountered much hard labor in esoterizing Krishna's sport with the gopīs, might have trouble with the explicit statement in their own chief canonical purāṇa the *Bhāgavata*

vedikāstāntriko miksha iti me trivibho makhaḥ trayānamīpsi-tenaivā vibhina mām samarcayeta

11.27.7

"My worship is of three kinds—Vedic, Tantrik, and mixed. A man should worship Me in whichever of these ways he prefers."

Even the *Bhāgavadgīta*, which in general equates creative "heat" with abstentive asceticism, but counsels moderation in austerity, sanctions the idea of a choice between the pursuit of Brahman without, against, or through the senses, according to personal bent:

"Some withdraw all their senses from external objects—for them, hearing and the other senses are the sacrifice and self-discipline the fire. Others let their mind and senses range freely, seeing Brahman in all external objects—for these, sound and other sense-objects are the offering, and the enjoyment of them is the fire."

Oceanic perception, in other words, can be favored either by total withdrawal of input or by "flooding," and the tapas which heats the alembic can be ascetic renunciation or intense passion—it is the dynamic and sometimes demonic Śiva who is Lord of Yoga. The first view renounces experience, the second sacramentalizes it—what neither condones is the superficial or the trivial; their censure is reserved for the "mere enjoyer" on one hand and the adage-cat ("letting I dare not wait upon I would") on the other. Viewed in this way, *brahmàcarya* means not anxious abstinence but Brahma-mindedness—the rejection of the secular as a category.

This sacramental use of experience, popularly preached in India by the Bauls, requires a more complex notion of "religion" than Ferenczi's analysis implies, but is anthropologically as common as asceticism. Orgiastic traditions put matters more robustly. The Tantrik *vīra*, for example, is a religious empiric and a devoted student of the fauna of numina, seeking comprehension of the boundaries of the Self by straightforward experimentation, in which he uses many of the traditional techniques normally applied by magicians to less philosophic ends—including chanting, fasting, ritualized taboo-breaking, and the active use of the senses, especially sexuality, with a single-mindedness and detachment from the usual employments of such means which is reminiscent of science rather than antinomian hedonism, the achievement of omnipotence, or its postulation elsewhere.

As to the content of the experience, "I am That" can mean that the self is a part of a transcendent whole, that man contains the divine, or that all the gods are inhabitants of our nervous system, according to taste. Tantriks are accordingly experimental Jungians. The vīra is concerned with experiences as an artist is with pictures, and his insights are esthetic, like Jung's or Blake's, though we can put a neurology and a psychosymbolism to them. By conscientiously freaking himself out he achieves "knowledge" in that both the I and the That are made to feel different and ultimately one—not by new facts, but rather by a reordered response to them based on altered ego-boundaries which can be genuinely novel. We can fit this kind of "religion," with labor, into a paradigm of recapitulated human individual ontogeny, and like all experimentation with the "self" it looks back to the fact that as altricial mammals our self developed slowly and in relation to parents who tend to reappear among the fauna of our heads (as animus, anima, the shadow self, and so on— the Tantrik objectifies many of these personages and studied their natural history long before Jung did). The face and identity which we give to the That or Those whose identity and personality we hypothecate will vary considerably—it may be sharply identified with some aspect of a parent or it may not.

There is an interesting critique of the Freudian concept of religious development *vis-à-vis* a more general view of its relation to self-experience in the "religion" of the Naskapi of Labrador. These people have no gods, ceremonies or tribal institutions, being isolated hunters in an exceptionally severe climate. They express their religious experience as being that of an internal friend, called "my friend" (Mista-peo) with whom dialog is had and from whom ethical and practical guidance are derived. The "friend" departs at or before death, and his departure signals this event.[34] This bears an interesting resemblance to the common hallucination of explorers in featureless landscapes that they have a companion, or an additional companion, sometimes identified with a conventional religious figure such as Christ or a saint, or the conviction of sailors in action that Drake or Nelson was present in spirit. We are familiar with the more general hallucinatory effects of reduced sensory input—this one appears to have connections originally with reduced social input whereby the self, or a component in it, is objectified as an echo, and is probably an important contributor to the spiritual effects of hermithood and retreat. I include it here to indicate that there is more to religious personalization than the identification of parent figures, and that parts of the Jungian internal fauna, such as the shadow self (which is usually negative in color) and the "great Man" (usually positive or standard-giving) have a biology which is experimentally investigable by the means, including sensory and social deprivation, which are traditional among experimental mystics.

VI.2
Charismatic experience

One reinforcer to such empirical religion lies in the social field.

A charismatic is someone whose self image has been altered by a peak experience. Not all such experiences are religious—they can equally be social: where they are religious, the subject usually expresses them socially (by an altered attitude to others, a zeal to proselytize) in a way which conveys that his boundaries are altered. This altering of boundaries, like moving the yard fence, makes the world look different, and conventional postures appear absurd. It does not take a shamanic vision or the Holy Grail to create charismatics. A simple instance may be seen among nudists. These are people who have found that the contradiction of a general convention is pleasurable, produces good psychological vibrations, and bonds them with others like-minded; any *homme moyen sensuel* who joins them will (a) feel embarrassed if he remains clothed and (b) leave the scene with an altered view of the prevailing convention—he will wonder why on earth everyone is so uptight about the normal body, and why they don't all live like that. This is a simple example of the charismatic transformation, showing two features common to many religious sources of charisma, namely sanctified taboo-breaking and bonding by means of a lay sacrament. When nudists were less acceptable, nudism shared a third common attribute of charismatic sects, namely secrecy.

Organized peak experiences, whether relatively trifling like this one or pretending to great depth and enlightenment, are an early feature of human religious behaviors: as soon as the shaman takes an initiate with him, or involves a group in ceremonial, alteration of self-image moves from the retail to the wholesale level, and may be facilitated here by group interaction: it is easier to freak out in company than alone. It is, moreover, dangerous to describe any such consciousness raising as trifling, even if it looks so to those on the outside looking in: the key ceremonies of many efficacious religions look trifling to the uninitiated, who accuse the initiates of stupidly reverencing inanimate objects or pieces of bread. There are wholly private springs of transformation—if the mystic's vision is really ineffable he may be tempted to give up the task of communicating it, though he more usually says, "You look too, and you will see what I mean." But in general we are here referring to an ingrained and very early character of human attempts at ego-boundary manipulation, that they are social, or communal, that they produce both insight and bonding between the inseers, and that the two feed each other. No human being is so sophisticated as to be quite unsusceptible to this socio-psychologic process; very emancipated people find unexpected reassurance in group nakedness, and Greek philosophers, hardly the most superstitious or credulous of people, found a profound peak experience in the Eleusinian Mysteries. What went on in these we do not know—Clement of Alexandria's account sounds like Billy Graham's idea of Esalen; he didn't approve, but hadn't been there. Their basis was a simple enough myth of the corn goddess, the seasons, and the wine god; there is no good evidence of any pharmacological assistance to the social and charismatic "trip," but it is a reflection of the size of the effect on educated and conventionally unreligious sceptics that not even Aristophanes made fun of Eleusis.

On the other hand, as Wasson[35] points out, it must have taken strong medicine to produce such an abiding impression of altered self in an audience of Greeks of all classes, not singly but in batches of two or three thousand. We may possibly have missed the point by concentrating on Dionysus the god of wine to the exclusion of Demeter the goddess of cereals. Ergot grows on several wild and cultivated forms of Mediterranean grain: magic cakes were part of the Eleusinian eucharist. We also know that Alcibiades caused a scandal by procuring some of them to use at a dissipated party. In the face of the Greek familiarity with theater, it is hard to imagine a purely dramatic presentation, however Freudian, which could have impressed a Greek audience on the scale of Eleusis—suggestion alone may have been enough, but one must suspect that some psychedelic agent assisted the efficacy of prayer.

VI.3
Sexual experience and the boundaries of self

Our charismatic behaviors, at least in California, tend to be relational and sexual rather than "religious"; in a culture which has made its institutional religion one of nonrelation and antisexuality nakedness may be literal or a more general symbol of Adamic nonpretence. One could discourse psychoanalytically on these (the unveiling of a phallus and a primal-scene hierogamy seem to have figured at Eleusis), but it is their social biology and their effect on the bounds of I, You and That which bears on the biology of religion, rather than the very varied means they have employed to disturb and hence re-form our sense of self.

Sexuality is central to religious behaviors either in its rejection, its magical transformation, or its sacramental acceptance. This, moreover, is sexuality in its everyday meaning, including coitus and orgasm, rather than its Freudian extension into symbolism. Most people, even in an antisexual religious tradition, intuit this connection. It could be so simply because sexuality is a central human concern, but the recognition of a connection between religion and our experience of identity suggests another, that coitus is almost the only ecstatic or fusional experience in the daily repertoire of even the most naive—"*la fouterie est le lyrisme du peuple*"—and the possibilities exist both that this is a reinforced experience easily expanded into other forms of action on the bounds of the I, and that the mechanism of the "oceanic experience" itself, also strongly rewarded at the cerebral level, belongs to, or uses the wiring of, the reward experience of orgasm.

Antisexual religions owe their rejection at the ideological level to different motives or rationalizations—Christianity to a general moralistic distaste for the pleasant, Gnosticism to the idea that it is evil to people an evil world (given the Pill, Gnostic antinomianism would have favored sexual activity simply as rule-breaking). Magicosexual ideologies often merge into the antisexual, but basically their concept is of a hydroelectric type sexual "energy" which should be conserved for mystical use ("sexual misers" in the terminology of Rawson for the semen-conserving Tantriks) or expended only occasionally on ceremonially orgiastic occasions: this is an archaic human assessment of the sexual, that by virtue of its power it should be treated as we treat radioactivity.

Charismatic and sacramentalizing religions start from a basic sexual polarity in the cosmos and attempt to generate similar energy by recreating or identifying with the divine Dyad (most left-hand Śaiva sects) or by generating erotic emotions such as tenderness (*śṛṅgāra*) and devotion (bhaktī) through sexual experience and transferring them from human partners to the divine, whose playfulness (līlā) becomes ours (the sexualizing Kṛṣṇa sects). Release from the bounds of arbitrary socio–sexual convention is, in effect, a partial moving of the bounds of I, which may be used either to acquire a knowledge of That, or, as in modern "human potential" experiences of the same kind, some of which contain elements convergent on both Śaiva and Vaiṣṇava *cakra-pūja*, to acquire knowledge of the I, in that removal of conventional fears and reservations releases new behaviors unfamiliar to the subject which then become available for reinforcement. Elements of more Freudian psychodrama are nearly always present, as they must be if at the same time the orgiastic experience is a relearning or reordering outside upbringing and the culture. Such Adamic or charismatic uses of sex, combining socialness, secrecy, or at least withdrawal from culture norms, and intense bonding among all the participants affect I-perception first by removing vulgar errors regarding our own acceptibility; second, by fusional-ecstatic experiences and heightened bonding (I–Thee, I–You, We), and finally by emergence with a greatly heightened social sense of personal reality and identity. In their secular form these are overriding effects: however overtly sexual they have a hidden agenda—often hidden from the participants—which is religious. In ritualized uses of the same behaviors, the theology takes over (a man may become both Śiva and Śaktī, or learn devotion to Kṛṣṇa experientially "before Whom all men are as women"), but the operant experiences are the same if the words expressing them are different.

Such religious uses of sexuality are unfamiliar to us and heretical in the Christian tradition (though quite frequent in past American history—witness the Oneida community and the Agapemonites). They now appear, or are appearing, in a secular–psychiatric form as part of the "sensitivity" or "human potential" movement, and may become domesticated, as indeed the *rās maṇḍala* of Kṛṣṇa has at times been; such behaviors are rightly to be seen as religious, not by analogy but homology—they have the same functions as theistic use of the same means.

Charismatic sexual yoga tends to begin in the area closest to our ordinary experience, that of "I–Thou–We", which is the area emphasized by modern secular exponents. This in itself can provide unexpected effects on I-ness, but it can also pass into the quite different mode characterized in the *Siddhamālarahasya* in which for each partner, if both are adepts, the other partner is an instrument; in which the I–Thou mode is deliberately limited by random choice of partner selected by drawing garments from a heap, and in which the socially inappropriate partner, in breach of caste or endogamy lines, is spiritually to be preferred. In the climactic experience the partners commence as He and She but wind up with each identifying both with Śiva and with Śakti.

We may not easily assimilate Tantrik usage in this culture, but the transition in any sexual yoga from I–Thou to I–That and from the interpersonal to the extrapersonal has a certain uncontrollable impetus of its own which experimenters with "open sexuality" are apt to encounter unawares. The inclination is naturally to stay with interpersonal explanations of its large mind-changing effects, because psychology is happier in this area than in any other. The efficacy of experimental religion does not, however, depend on the insight of the participants into what they are doing.

Californians and others entering a secular rās maṇḍala type experience simply out of curiosity or in pursuit of sexual kicks have on occasion found the anthropological efficacy of the rite disturbing, in that the "hidden agenda" takes over, and experiences of innocence, bonding or disquieting self-confrontation predominate over the salacious or the exciting, for which they originally came. Oddly enough this phenomenon does not contradict the sizable consensus against "sex" found among professional mystics, even though some of these, like other citizens, reject such experiments, chiefly through prudery, tradition or both. It is in sharp contrast to the spiritual non-efficacy of irregular sexuality played according to the general rules of the culture—clandestine adultery, "hot" sex generally: this distinction may be what is stressed in the differences between the mystagogic unions in the upper bands of the Khājuraho temple sculptures and the goings-on, sometimes interpreted as the "hot" or purely secular couplings of the paśu (unenlightened) in the lower. It is not, as the saying goes, what you do—it's the way that you do it. This type of charismatic enactment has a particular appropriateness in our own culture, not only because we have rediscovered sexuality, but because it is about the only source of immediate charisma to which we seem at all readily open.

It is not impossible that the singular efficacy of sexual *koinonia*, whether ritual or private, as a form of yoga leading to inward perception of That may have been one of the reasons that Christianity, and before that Judaism, were so condemnatory of it. Both religions strongly objectify God and contrast him with man as creature. The accusations of holding charismatic sexual rites leveled at early Christians by moralistic pagans could well have been true, and the rapid promotion of a strongly contrasting cult of celibacy, chastity, and the rejection even of nonsexual behaviors which were pleasant may have arisen not only from standard human anxieties but from conflict between theology and a sense of inner deity which, because internal in fallen man, must be a delusion of the enemy—especially since the means of attainment was shared with some at least of the competing pagan mysteries. If God is to be objectified, and indwelling in us only through grace, then any secular means of ecstasy which makes the location of That internal, particularly when it chimes with a whole series of pre-existent moral anxieties and the breaking of social taboos, is a terribly frightening thing, making us wonder, as Aldous Huxley did, whether we are not being deluded, through "lust" which was already, in its "hot" form, disreputable to the solid citizen, into worshipping ourselves. There were, no doubt, other factors in the near-lunatic antisexuality of some early Christian (and later Hindu) sadhus, but in the case of the Christians, who were in the process of developing an intellectual structure to systematize what was in origin a cult based on bhakti, this one may well have played a greater part than rewritten church history now suggests.

Surajit Sinha[36] describes the influence in a Vaisnava village of two successive sages representing two Krsna traditions: one puritan; the other not. The first sadhu devoted much preaching to sin, hell, and their avoidance, equating sin with the unspirituality arising from loss of semen, and enjoining teetotalism and vegetarianism. The second was in the habit of singing a song which ran:

> "Sing the name of Hari;
> Take chicken curry
> And the lap of a young woman . . ."

The village "listened with relief" to this less ascetic view. Both sadhus taught the conventional *ratisadhan* (intercourse with the conservation of semen and "absorption of the female seed")— neither approached the conventional Christian assessment of sexuality. One can, of course, offer Freudian interpretations of both emphases; but in contrast to the Freudian myths discovered by Róheim in Australia, the fit is a partial and not a particularly easy one; no prohibitive parent is objectified, even in the person of Yama, the god of retribution.

There are accordingly several sexual-religious archetypes: in the rejecting systems pleasure is forbidden fruit because it tends to internalize the divine experience; and parental prohibition and jealousy are projected on God, the classic Freudian pattern. In a second, the cosmos is dyadic, and the coition of the human dyad generates ecstasy by identification in the same way as the coition of the cosmic dyad "powers" creation: we identify with the Primal Scene. In a third, sexual release is dramatized by withdrawal from cultural taboos, and the resulting charismatic bonding dramatizes the brotherhood of humans in the ecstatic experience. Brotherhood in this case is anthropologically correct, for the sharing of women by men is phylogenetically a brotherly, and of men by women, a sisterly, experience persisting fully in only a few traditions, but once possibly general, and larvally present in the background of Hinduism where Draupadī is married to all the Pāndavas and the younger brother (*dewar*) has rights with the elder sister-in-law (*bhaujī*), even if these are now teasing rather than frankly sexual.[37] This pattern represents a charismatic levirate.

Goddesses belong to the second two patterns—to the patristic religions they are dangerous and disgusting, and require to be sterilized by virginity. In the oldest human traditions, which saw woman as the possessor of the magic of making new people, while being alarmingly in touch with cosmic matters such as lunar cyclicity, the mother outranks the father in theogonies. Later working of this material may make the male immanent, but the female is the initiatrix—she is the stone from which the spark is struck, and moreover, the only portable and domestic source of dissociative ecstasy for male sages as for the paśu or naive believer: "*buddhatvaṁ yoṣityoṇisamāśritam*," "enlightenment is in the vulva of woman," "*maithunena mahāyogi mama tulyo na saṁśaya*"—"in coitus I am not distinct from the Great Yogi [Śiva]."

The importance of these patterns would appear, as we shall see, to lie in their connection with individuation. One part of the genesis of adult identity is concerned with division from the mother—not only as an abstraction of physical birth, but in the discovery of separateness which renders incorporation threatening. For the male, this separation is double, since it involves also incorporation of a contrasting gender role and a re-approach to the female in mating which involves a dramatized reincorporation. Vast tracts of religious behaviors, in so far as they touch on identity and our experience of it, appear to be subsumed here—Freudian constructs, such as the castrating mother to whom the penis must be surrendered and who returns it flaccid, "shrinking the organs of life so that they become finite and herself infinite" (Blake), and cosmologic analogies in which the mother is identified with the earth and *a fortiori* with the body image or some of its aspects. Dyadic yogas act out many of these milestones or states on the road to adult individuation, projecting them into cosmology (and explaining why we see aspects of the cosmos as we do): charismatic sexual yogas recreate benign regres‍sion by levelling sexuality for the nonce with childhood play, and taking the projection from there. We need only look at this richness of overdetermination to question any formula as simplistic as that of Ferenczi. At the same time sexuality does have an integral—I almost wrote "seminal"—connection with the biology of religious behaviors going beyond the crude projection of prohibitive parents envisaged by Freud in his approach to the type of religion with which he was familiar.

Existential arguments in which religion is defined as a group of behaviors connected with the delimiting of the boundaries of "self," although they appeal to philosophers, and to psychiatrists engaged in sorting out the practical identity problems of patients, assort rather ill with analysis of actual mechanisms. Self is an experience, not an object: we can infer how it feels in others by introspection, but not very far (*what*, neurologically speaking, is happening when I determine to move my thumb, and what is the structure of the I which is experienced as determining? Where, in other words, does the environment start?). It is, however, a compelling experience, and we almost certainly share some components of it with social animals, though the argument is otiose in view of the impossibility of ascertaining how it feels to be a dog or a chimpanzee. Altered states of consciousness, especially those concerned with alteration or manipulation of the body image, in one manner, and sexual experiences in another, certainly are able to affect the way in which this experience goes. They seem to have the effect of altering the position of the fence around experienced identity, which is almost certainly, in part, a complex of learned reactions, so as to take in, or exclude, things formerly outside or inside, while the very fact of so doing shakes up our impression of where "we" begin or end *vis-à-vis* the not-I. Some of these states seem to involve specific neurological manipulations—all of them disturb the kind of mentalism our culture favors: or, if you prefer, they increase the range of mental behaviors we display, so that new ones become available for reinforcement.

We can see, accordingly, that the religious behaviors we can observe (the only substrate for any talk about a biology of religion) have to do with the odd and elusive human experience of the Self, with the fact that others have selves to which we are programmed to relate, and that since all that is not Self is Other, there is an overwhelming temptation to infer that the Other has an experience of Self too.

VI.4
Asceticism, masochism and identity

Behaviorists and non-behaviorists would probably be of one mind that the homuncular mode, even if it be programmed, is basically learned (so that a robot brain, if it had not been exposed to human ontogeny, might not show it in a typically human form). Skinner[38] makes the illuminating point that most I-ness learning is negative or connected with punitive experience, which sets our boundaries: learning by reinforcement is largely learning unawares. It is discomfort rather than a sense of well-being which is the individuating experience: I "know" my toe as distinct only when it hurts.

A positive sense of I-ness with well-being (*sahāja*), reflecting the ongoing effects of past oceanic experiences, has been cultivated by yogas, particularly Tantrik yogas, but Skinner's formulation offers one possible mechanism for the "bliss" component of nonhomuncular experience—it reflects a total reminiscence of reinforcing experience beside being (though Skinner would disclaim the language) a specifically pre-Edipal reminiscence. There would be a strong suspicion psychoanalytically that I-ness of the punitive or restrictive kind is learned during Edipal learning, and that ecstatics in general and sexually-promoted ecstasies in particular specifically reverse this group of conditionings, were it not that at another level most ecstatics seem to keep their sexual anxieties intact, and even treat excessive anxiety and prohibition as if they were preconditions of the nonhomuncular experience, so that *brahmācarya*, which means "going or wandering in the sphere of Brahman" has been translated by generations of sadhus as "monastic chastity," and "chastity" has been perverted by some Christians to mean simply abstinence.

In nearly all archaic human traditions we find the concept of "ordeal" associated with the acquisition of magical powers. This use of "austerities" (self-testing, discomfort, infliction), expressed in Sanskrit by *tapāsya* (the plural of *tapas*, heat) is not properly masochism, if by masochism we mean the pursuit of discomfort, pain or humiliation for its own sake. On the other hand, it is arguable from observation whether the overtly sexual masochist—who requires to be flogged in order to reach orgasm, for example—is pursuing discomfort "for its own sake." In most instances he is not. We have tended to look, in both the religious and the sexual context, to self-punitive motives, and in both cases they are not rarely present, at

98

least as original sources of the notion behind the behavior; it could equally be true that there are athletes who undergo extreme tapāsya, and would-be astronauts who volunteer for dangerous and unpleasant training, rather to propitiate inner guilt than because of the effects on performance, and yet the performance may justify the rationalization. The point is that tapāsya of the traditional kinds prescribed respectively for sexual, mystical or athletic purposes produce effects on performance and experience in these fields *per se*, which transcend the conscious or unconscious object which led an individual to adopt them. Thus wholly penitential flagellation can produce embarrassingly secular orgasm, and people whose motives in undertaking ascetic or masochistic exercises were probably sexual may find themselves experiencing altered consciousness of a non-sexual character.

Religious ordeals are unpopular in our culture, as we are shocked by the notion that Boot Camp produces better soldiers. In fact athletic performance and sexual arousal are now the only settings in which we can observe the specific effects of tapāsya without being made uncomfortable about them—a striking reversal.

One is tempted to see asceticism as a purely cultural outgrowth of the mystical undertaking, and pathological at that, being based on the fact that those who most fear their own I-ness most want to get rid of it, but askesis does not necessarily involve masochism, and the testimony is fairly unanimous, even among those who reckon that their exercises no more than facilitate, rather than reliably produce, changes in I-experience. Thus even frankly orgiastic yogas enjoin discipline of a negatively reinforced kind, and even avoid orgasm in the specific mystical use of sexuality, though this is rationalized physiologically as "conserving semen." It may be that the negatively reinforced I can be treated like a phobia and "flooded" by pushing negative reinforcement or frankly aversive inputs to a point where the system breaks down. Couple this with the disorientating effect of tapāsya such as fasting, immobility and sensory deprivation, and the ascetic recipe begins to make sense—it is not a necessary condition of unconventional I perception, any more than is the taking of LSD, but those who have practiced it—like the masochist Heinrich Suso quoted by William James—from quite other, and probably sexual, motives, found empirically that altered I-states followed. The bizarre recipe for aversive self-treatment given by St John of the Cross passes with agility from "seeking that which is most distasteful" to a validly mystical formula ("So as to be all things, be willing to be nothing") and from thence into diction prefiguring what sounds very like orgasm, a sequence which gives us some of the operants of the nirvīkalpa mode of perception, though not yet the exact roles which they play. Evidently it can be triggered by austerity, or by displaced sexuality, the two reinforcing each other in some mystics as in many nonmystics—indeed, there are few of the physical dodges and attacks on the body image which are used to achieve magical or mystical states which are not also used by some people and traditions to achieve the secular mystical experience of heightened orgasm.

"Masochism" in its sexual context is so heavily overdetermined, involving physical stimulation, elements drawn from general dominance-behaviors and carried over into sex, and concepts built on infantile ideas of guilt and punishment at the Freudian level, that most psychiatrists would be glad to drop it altogether, distinguishing "programmed plays" (which heighten sexual arousal), anxiety-appeasing rituals which act as transitional objects (in the manner of a teddy-bear or a beloved piece of blanket) and genuinely self-destructive behaviors. The trouble is that any or all of these may coexist, so that one man's playfulness is another man's disability. Something very similar applies to the masochisms of the religious—what started as pathological self-punishment may unexpectedly lead to religious rather than sexual arousal, and what has been taught by sadhus as a means of heightening religious arousal (abstinence, discomfort, sensory deprivation, and tapāsya generally) will naturally appeal to the pathologically anxious and self-punitive whether or not they lead to fusional experience. Add to this that sexual arousal is fusional, though not all fusional experiences are sexual, and we come the full circle and can enter the continuous performance at any point. It is all very complicated. What is clear is that if many serious sadhus engage in masochistic-looking austerities, they do not do it for kicks, or not for the same kicks as the "masochist"—though one variety of kick is in certain respects linked to the other.

The techniques used in sexual and mystical manipulation of the body image, with a view to "collapsing" it into a dissociative or oceanic perception, are certainly overdetermined. In spite of the richness of associations with childhood experience, human psycho-sexual preoccupations, and social phenomena such as dominance, aggression and submission, they may be effective in practice for neurological reasons. The constant reappearance in anthropology, mystical exercises and sexual techniques of specific stimuli such as body-image confusion, forced immobility, painful stimulation, and concentration on skin textures and their modification (which underlies many idiosyncratic sexual releasers—fetishes) may be more closely related to the experiments of von Bekesy[39] on simultaneous stimulation than to Freudian psychosymbolism and infantile reminiscence alone. We depend on the conventional body image to keep the "I" internal and the external distinct from it, and these methods circumvent the conventional body image and reduce the stereoscopic effect on which I-ness seems to depend.

In our society, charismatic and initiatory yogas directed to sexual ends constitute the only spontaneous magico-religious rituals of I-manipulation which we can observe. It might seem odd to classify the sexual rituals of so-called sadomasochists as "religious," but their anthropological relation to traditional magic is close. So far it has usually been studied from the wrong end (by classing magical operations as sadomasochistic) rather than by treating purported sexual rituals as genuinely magical—a distortion which the participants often promote by adopting the common psychiatric valuation of their behaviors and enacting charades in conformity with it.

The relationship of the manipulating or "top" partner to the manipulated or "bottom" partner, when we actually observe it, belies the content of the charade which may be played—it is not in fact that of dominator or master to dominated or slave, but that of facilitator or psychopomp, who uses control to evoke, to push into transcendent experience—almost exactly that of coach to athlete or platoon commander to recruit. Like the coach or the commander, the manipulator "compels" the manipulated into states or performances of which the manipulated did not know themselves to be capable, but the compulsion is skilful facilitation, since the states evoked represent only the expression of potentials already present. Often the only function of the charades is to give coherence and superficial meaning to the "game," which is exactly analogous to any other training-game depending on evocation and psyching-out the trainee, who may be in the event experientially enhanced, not humiliated, by the total experience. In reality the "top" partner is psychologically the more passive, since he or she appears to act as an externalized projection of the "bottom" partner, or some component of their identity actively externalized, an extraordinary form of reified transference. The embodiment of externalized selves for the use of others—the clients or initiates—is a conventional but neglected role both of the shaman or initiator and of the psychotherapist; this is one of its most striking modern forms. That the ritual is in this case sexual and the overt objective sexual arousal is in line with our lack of dissociative experiences outside the sexual field, but as with so many overtly sexual experiments—"open" or group sexuality being another, there is a hidden agenda which is not sexual so much as magical or magico-religious, and which tends to take over.

This ethological interpretation is not so far at variance with the Freudian view as might appear. The charade overtly or covertly includes reminiscences of punitive individuation, and the recapitulation of these in order to "get behind" them facilitates the recreation of a pregenital, non-individuated experience. In magic, however, as opposed to symptomatic sadomasochism, ordeals represent not a continuing appeasement of guilt by infliction, but rather a form of initiation or ongoing *rite de passage*: the singularity of this, compared with other more social *rites de passage*, is that it is a backward-running initiation, into pre-Edipal experience. Merlin, the chief yogic wizard of Celtic tradition, was born an old man and died an infant, a highly significant myth. In shamanic traditions "acting backwards" is a source of magical power, beside being a denial of the unidirectionality of Time, which, as we have seen, is probably a structural consequence of the mechanics of I-ness. The naive masochist who is turned on by being treated as a baby undergoing the aversive phase of individuation may accordingly be onto an anthropological and magical maneuver of greater power than he realizes.

If one in fact examines, rather than psychoanalyzes, the actual practices of people who—in the modern climate of public sexual confession—profess themselves to be "into S and M," one will find that these commonly have very little to do with sadomasochism and a great deal to do with body-image manipulation: they are using ordeal as a means of altering identity boundaries—in this case pursuit of sexual orgasm at a heightened level—tight fettering, sensory depriv-ation, postponement, mild pain and occasionally an element of fear. Drumming, dancing and loud noise, which are not "masochistic," are similarly active in inducing both sexual and mystical self-alteration. These techniques are precisely those used traditionally in shamanic arousal—but guilty people will also use tapāsya, or acts interpretable as punitive, in expiation, and self-destructive people as a means of self-mischief. Reich's percipient view of the masochist as one who wants to transcend or explode the body image—to burst, in fact—and who may assault the boundaries of the actual body in doing so, applies almost equally patly to the mystic, who wishes to implode the illusion of identity. The ego being a body ego, attacks on the body image seem to be built in to this process physiologically: and the ordeals imposed on themselves by those whose motives, like those of St Simeon Stylites, were almost certainly self-punishing at a psychoanalytic level may in fact produce the other types of experience for which nonpathologic mystics undertake them. In Roman society, where overt, pathologic sadism was an institutionalized public entertainment, the singular ordeal of the Villa of the Mysteries with its frightened and flagellated initiate exhibits the other use of such apparently punitive behaviors.

Indeed, we can go further, and recognize in genuine sadomas-ochism the pathological misreading of the magico-sexual use of "ordeal" to manipulate I-ness. The sadomasochist interprets it as hostility in the service of anxiety and guilt, and expresses that hostility in sexual cruelty: to the legitimacy of magic directed at the body image he opposes a sorcery which attempts to hijack or force the magic in mitigation of personal insecurity and disturbance. This closely resembles the child's misreading of the "primal scene," where vigorous coition is read as a hostile act, and hostility may be attached to the concept of the sexual or of love itself. De Sade and Gilles de Rais were such misguided sorcerers—the truly punishing or self-punishing saints, the sore-covered ascetics and flagellants and the Inquisitors, represent the religious wing of this deviation. We can learn more of this interaction from J.-K. Huysmans, perhaps, than from a psychoanalysis which, like the child seeing its parents in coition, misses the legitimate significance of behaviors which have a biology; such analysis draws its interpretation from patients who similarly misread them and endanger themselves and others in consequence. Masochists may assault the body image, but attempts to manipulate the body image amounting almost to assault are not a sufficient criterion of masochism. We see them in the athlete, the lover, and the mystic also.

VII.1
Archetypes and the spiritual fauna

It is the most important contribution of Jung to the psychoanalysis of religion that in his view, though perhaps not in his detailed development, a key to the religious experience of "self" can be found in what I would term the fauna of religious formulation—the objectified personages and numina which mythologies postulate to fit their intellectual or experiential needs, portions of self-experience which are disembodied because not included in the largely arbitrary I. Coming from a monotheistic tradition, we easily neglect the examination of these as superstitious and intellectually unimportant; but that is because we objectify God and give him an importance in cosmology.

The only cosmology to which these personage-archetypes are relevant is the "cosmology" of our own heads. So far from being arbitrary personifications of natural forces (the traditional Judaeo-Christian idea of "idols"), the personages which religious meditants encounter, in traditions which do not limit themselves doctrinally to one god plus assorted saints, are part of the structure of human inner space, reflections, as it were, from the close interplay of neurology, self-experience, and culture. They represent experiences arising from the character of our pattern-generating and pattern-receiving system, which must be at some point closely coupled to the experience of "self"; portions of the "self" temporarily observed or extruded. Some are Freudian, or capable of Freudian interpretation—not surprisingly, in view of the importance of this matrix in early psychosexual experience; but they cannot, as Jung first pointed out, all be boiled down to *mūrtis* of Mother Goddess, Daddy Edipus, and the Child, though commonly these figures are evident in or at least among them. Many are, by their consistency, straight reflections off parts of our pattern-forming system, and important because aspects of the structure of that system can be inferred from them, as molecular structure not otherwise visible can be inferred from an X-ray scatter picture.

Even in a strongly objectifying theology such as that of Christian orthodoxy, and even in an objectifying and monistic theology such as Judaism, the multiplicity of our experience of self, as well as its unity, are reflected in God. In a sense the Trinity represents a reflection of a two-part "self" giving rise to a spiritual third person, while the *Kabbalah* specifically attributes to God three faces, arranged like those on a totem-pole.

No serious anthropologist would now argue that "myths" spring fully armed from the head, or the Jungian unconscious, of any period—more often they are explanatory accounts of social phenomena or projections which imply that human actions have counterparts in the macrocosm which validate them. As to the inner fauna of the minds which repeat or elaborate the myths, their content is in no sense "transcendent" or part of any *ur*-unconscious—it is quite manifestly programmed, like other content-features of our sense of identity, by social pattern: animus and anima, for example, embody in Jung's usage an entire crop of presuppositions about gender roles common in our society. Stories and rites which originated in an ambience of matriarchy and calendar-rites can be turned stern-on in sense when repeated later in a context of patriarchy and kingship, with king-like gods in place of cosmic goddesses. On the other hand, like Gilbert and Sullivan's operas, major myths give a strong impression of having been written for a single cast of singers to perform, and it is this cast which consists of reflections from the I-ness of the individual. Human family structure, and outside that human tribal and social structures, assign the roles, but the *dramatis personae* remain the same. There are, in fact, only a limited number of schemata which can express ordered social or ordered physical cosmos and which are at the same time click-fits with the structure of internal perception. These are the authentic archetypes, and, as Jung points out, they are contentless, or capable of receiving almost any content—they are preferred ways of objectifying structure.

Such archetypes have clearly a hardnosed psychobiology of their own. To regard them as arbitrary products of human fancy is to neglect a source of information, and is as naive as to take them seriously as comments on real cosmology. Their archetypal character invests such figures with a "rightness," however much their objectification offends our rationalism, and this rightness exists for exactly the already-stated reason that a waffle fits a waffle-iron—they are products of our self-experience. This fit can carry disabling conviction and reinforce irrational or arbitrary cosmologies; but it is notable that sophisticated observers and users of the faunas of numina, as opposed to naive believers, have in all traditions recognized their true significance. In the Tantrik version of Hinduism, which is the most experientially empirical of all its versions, "Man is himself Brahman"[40] and hence all the lower numina of a huge pantheon are similarly internal. The numina of the Valentinian Gnostic pleroma were objectified, but there are hints here that man is "father of all, and his first name is Man," so that even the Archons and angels, who oppress him in creation under the illusion that they are themselves gods, are in some sense human emanations[41] whose real field of operations is the microcosm rather than the cosmos as such. We have a modern example of such objectification in the later work of Reich, where valid inner processes become reified as new forms of physical energy at a semi-delusional level. In a shamanic culture, such things would have been projected as spirits with less tragic consequences.

Oddly enough the most comprehensive explorer of this aspect of mystical objectification is not Jung but Blake—possibly the only member of our culture to give his religion-making and fauna-describing intuitions full rein. Blake's pleroma or Divine Family of multiple, alarming, passionate numina, all with numerous forms, numerous emanations, Śaktīs or female counterparts, sons, shadow-selves and servants on a scale to boggle even Hindu theogony, live in a cosmos parallel to the objective, and are, explicitly, states of man-Albion, who originally included the whole of the universe (not surprisingly, since it is the universe of human inner experience and pattern-perception). This is Gnosticism psychologized, though Blake would have treated this formulation with insult and called his fauna-making Divine Imagination. Even the fierce and unmanageable Archons, the Zoas—of whom Urizen-Satan, inventor of sin, law-and-order and the Great Selfhood is one—and figures like the Shadow Female or Nameless Mother who spins the obscuring veil Ulro from her bowels on the model of the Gnostic Sophia spinning a screen between the Universe and the Divine, under cover of which the journeyman Archons produce a faulty Creation around divine Man—all are, if one reads Blake's development of them carefully, consciously aspects not of outer, but of a parallel inner, cosmology. The only problem for such mysticism is how far microcosm really fits macrocosm, and how far outer and "inner" cosmology fit each other—not an anti-scientific question, when one considers how much our inner pattern-analyzing mechanism determines the outer patterns we detect.

We are now seeing a resurgence of every kind of uncritical use of archetypes, fueled to a large extent by a long tradition of religious literalism and monotheism—the archetypes fill needs and have uses; but one of those uses is certainly not to supersede objective cosmology. What we are facing is the need now to apply rational analysis to the human "computer," one of whose products is identity-sense, and another this plethora of relevant but nonliteral images. Superstition consists in treating them literally, in which case they are simply misleading. We would seem in fact to be due for an exploration of "inner space" as painstaking as our exploration of outer; but while Blake was right in thinking that this can only be done imaginatively and not in terms analogous to Newtonian physics, the significances we give to what we find ourselves imagining can now be made the subject of objective analysis, even though the needs they meet cannot always be so analyzed explicitly. Once it is recognized that all theologies and cosmologies are descriptions of man, not of God or gods, and that one That with which the I engages in dialog is the inner That of the human nervous system and its software, the religious uses of such things become clearer.

While the Tantrik recognizes without disturbance that in a peak experience he is himself Brahman, minds from a tradition with a harder view of the difference between inner and outer cosmologies find the idea distressing, and ground for suspecting that the oceanic sensation is in some way spurious. So Aldous Huxley, under the influence of LSD and dilaudid during his terminal illness, had visions of universal Buddhahood in which he himself nonetheless was the "star"—"It was an insight, but at the same time the most dangerous of errors . . . inasmuch as one was worshipping oneself."[42] Not, perhaps, "worshipping," but certainly experiencing, through what Jung terms positive expansion—without specific input, what, after all, beside "oneself" could there be to experience in a wholly endogenous event? Zaehner[43] points out the disturbing effect on objectifying religions of "the implication that the personal God they claim to experience in faith does not really exist because many Hindus and most Buddhists do not experience him in this way at all, but claim to experience him, or rather 'it,' immediately in the innermost core of their being." In fact the recognition that naive objectification of That is as much an illusion as the naive if inbuilt objectification of I is almost the hallmark of sophisticated religious mysticisms—even occasionally in the Christian tradition, ranging from the Inner Light of Quakerism to Meister Eckhart's dictum that the final renunciation is when man for God's sake takes leave of God. The analytic enteroception required for the cultivation of mystical states sharpens our expertise in dealing with parts of our own identity so that the nature of the experience is perceived without being taken to devalue it.

Literalism and historicism, useful as they are, have actually made us lose sophistication in dealing with this inner-cosmological experience. Inner-cosmology is at least as immediate as outer, and nearer home: we *see* the sky and ask, like O'Casey's Paycock, "What is the stars?" but the intuitive answers come from inner cosmology. Innerly sophisticated orders, like the Aborigines', recognize a dream state and a dream time having their own structures, related to the objective "outside" on which they comment, and which they organize, but not identical with it—so that rocks both "are" rocks and "are" the bones of a mythical ancestor in the dream time. Inner cosmology is also a source of much matter for philosophy, if not for obfuscation, in that one archetypally appealing idea, and an objectively "true" one as well, is that man both "makes" the inner-space world (it would not exist if he did not), and is made by it (he would not exist if it did not—moreover, since it is part of him, the separateness from which of the I-experience is an appearance or illusion, it is through the pattern-mechanism implicit in it that all dialog, except dialog with the pattern-mechanism itself, must be had).

We see more clearly here at the biological than at the existential philosophical level how "religious" and all other human experience is heavily imprinted with the ambiguity caused by our objective identity sense—objective in the sense that it depends on and is part of cerebral machinery, but does not feel as if it were; it has to objectify by treating the machinery as other, subjective structure as objective, and even itself as a manifestation of a noncorporeal soul (even this is paradoxical and becomes elaborated: for the Gnostics, soul, spirit and identity were three distinct things). In fact, if we define the scientific revolution as the skill of distinguishing inner from outer structure, we still encounter the problems in Wallace Stevens's poem (see p. 31).

More interesting still, to a biologist, is that the "structures" occurring in a tradition-based form in Hinduism, in an experiential form in shamanic visions, and in a literary–imaginative form in Blake or Yeats with gleanings from tradition (Swedenborg, Gnosticism, Hinduism) thrown in, are apparently mental "organs," bits of the self lying near the Self–Other boundary which we arbitrarily set but can vary. They must reflect both brain structure and culture structure, but these are evolved and adaptive, and presumably so are they; and so is the tendency to form them. The long period of zoistic culture which we assume, probably rightly, to have been spent by preliterate man was very probably a period when these mental tricks—disadaptive if one wants to study particle physics, but relevant even when we start to philosophize about the objective validity of structures—were highly adaptive. At that time ceremony was as important for survival as we now think objective science to be. There is, moreover, no way of getting rid of them. Jungian maṇḍalas, with a whole rack of *interiora* arising from them, are built into the projection of the retina, but they model out in our circular structures for the universe, for the atom and elsewhere with credible correspondence to the objective. What exactly this trick of projecting or objectifying parts of the mind as Other adapted us to, and why it remains on the program, it is difficult to do more than guess by jobbing backward, but as with the capacity to dissociate into shamanic visions it quite possibly had something to do with the need to relate to the environment and to other social humans similarly endowed through compelling structural patterns carrying, upon compliance, the rewards of "rightness" or "fit."

Psychosymbolic interest, and even pre-psychoanalytic interest dating from Frazer, have tended to concentrate on explicit structures in religious thinking which have a manifest social content plus some familial or Freudian reference to human developmental experience—the Dying God as Son, for example—precisely the story-type religious structures with which our own culture is most familiar and religiously at ease. The "superstitious" or "idolatrous" formulations culturally more remote from us are, however, bio-psychologically by far the more interesting. They may, and do, acquire Freudian or cultural color, but appear nevertheless to represent a shorthand for inner experiences of a very fundamental kind.

> "The great traditional mystical symbolisms are spontaneously rediscovered by modern men in dreams, hallucinations and pathological ecstasies, including those induced chemically. The community of pattern crosses boundaries of race and time which we might have thought were impassable. In view of what has just been said, this means that they should be taken seriously, for it is among them that we are likely to discover the originating formulae which make us men-in-a-world."[44]

Also, one might add, we may find a number of clues, or at least possible lines of investigation, into the nature of the human identity experience *vis-à-vis* the body image and the interaction of this with our cosmology. Unfortunately for a science of religion in line with other biologies they are subjectively perceptible only—it has taken the vogue for meditation plus the (hard-centered) documentation of biofeedback to overcome unease at the quite imaginary ambiguity between the anatomical account of the "subtle-body" of Tantrik yoga and the observable and dissectable body. Once seen as a shorthand (*kalpanatmika*—"imaginary" or "virtual", Patañjali calls it) for inner body image manipulations (which even in the simple case of vascular control we can still not verbalize in our own, Gray's-anatomical, terms) the ambiguity is recognized as the scientoid equivalent of the Victorian conviction that Hindus "worship idols." Once experienced, we can go on in hard-nosed fashion to work out exactly what they mean in terms of wiring, that being the mode of our culture, and a productive one never before applied to this archaic material.[44]

Another contrasting feature both of religions and of their philosophic offshoots since Plotinus has been monism and search for the "One" (even in the case of religions which, like Hinduism, stress the power of the One to express itself in as many forms as it chooses). It may or may not be sound to see in this human obsession with underlying unity the projection of our own experience of our identity as "one" and the disturbing effect of any condition in which the self is perceived as multiple, but it is at least tempting. If the guess is correct, it provides another reason for looking for links between the identity experience of humans and the behaviors we class as religious. Science no less than theology and ontogeny is profoundly bothered by conflicting paradigms in, for example, physics, though mathematics seems reconciled to the idea that no language can be at once univocal and without system breaks. Religion sometimes contrives to allay this kind of worry and permit key-changes in thinking through the experience of diverse selves—shamanism certainly does—but systematized religion has moved away from any such tendency except where mystics are concerned, and they have dealt in dvaita as a "path" to a more desirable advaita perception which even fuses the self experience with the One, thereby short-circuiting diversity altogether. In all this the only thing which appears common is the human identity sense as starting point for an entire range of structures.

Similar forces lead the Australian Aborigine, who is culturally an adept in the exploration of the I–not-I antithesis, to objectify his personal and social identity in a concrete object, the *churunga*, inscribed with maṇḍalas, acquired at puberty, and placed at his death in a fissure of the rocks with the churungas of his people, a given "identity" socially confirmed. *Rites de passage* are not automatically religious, but religions tend to involve them as they delimit social transformation in the clothing, as it were, of the I, the external roles required of it. In fact the component of sociality in religious behaviors, so much stressed by modern and pre-modern ethicists, who would reject Eleusis on the ground that it promised immortality to an initiated burglar but not to righteous Epaminondas, is in fact probably stronger at the level of the trivial and primitive than at the level of the ethical and philosophical.

VII.2
Individuation and cosmology

Pre-scientific cosmologies, those which antedate the "religion of objectivity," are not as a rule histories of the Universe, imaginative or otherwise, but metaphors for individuation, the process by which each individual "creates" an objective world. The derivation from I–That as the basis of objectivizing reality fits reasonably well, not only with their detail, which often looks exotic but is very rarely arbitrary, but also with their penchant for monism followed by a creation based on limitation or division of the One—which is very much what does occur in individual development as the Cartesian I and other members of the internal fauna acquire identity. Some details, if one cares to take the trouble, are potentially Freudian, though this is probably a minor overdeterminant compared with social ambivalence toward the general magical attributes of woman. In the typical version the One "took no pleasure in being alone" and created a mate from his own substance (thereby himself acquiring gender). It is this female element which then sets about creating diversity, either by simple coition and fertility or (in the Gnostic version) by a hubristic and liberated attempt to go it alone, which has created most of our problems of Illusion. Buddhism is out of line in transposing the sex roles and making the male creative and the female passive.

Bearing in mind which Universe they are talking about, it is interesting to look in greater detail at some of these myths, their conformity with normal individuation, and the means they recommend to reverse or unscramble it in the pursuit of original undifferentiated perception.

The "illusion" (maya) conceived of both by Gnosticism and by Hinduism as generative of the perceived universe is, at root, the illusion of I-ness, the homuncular illusion from which we began this examination, the sensation or experience of individual existence (*āsmat*), from which categories spring. It affects both man and, apparently, Brahman: "none can see me surrounded by the illusion of identity."[45] Both man and projected divinity express identity in the three propositions "*aham ajñaḥ, mām aham na jānāmi, tvām aham na jānāmi*": "I am the unknown, I do not know myself, I do not know you." Similarly, in the Hindu view, with monotheism or monism— "God" is something a great deal more complex than a person or force, exactly as the worshipper, however vividly he feels himself to be an I, is actually something less arbitrary and more complex— something in each case more like a locus than an object or point, and capable of varying inclusion and exclusion. "The notion of divine unity is therefore a fiction, a mental construction which is merely a projection of the living notion of individuality . . . a shaping of "god" to the image of Man."[46] One is virtually compelled to raid Sanskrit for a terminology in these matters which are critical to the definition of religion. Christianity has examined them only in disputation over the dual identity of Christ, and has borrowed the emphatic monism *Adonai elohenu Adonai echad* only with this reservation, which is not the point which Hindu and Gnostic theology are making. The closest Catholic approach to the I–That relation is possibly the debate over active and infused contemplation.

Tantrik and Gnostic cosmologies are more typical in sharing the ideas of an original One, division of the One into sexual poles, and the creation of diversity through illusion by the activity of the female polar principle. These are not "cosmologies" in our sense of being accounts of creation—what they are is accounts of inner or introspective experience: the "cosmos" to which they refer is the human self, the Giant Albion—explicitly represented in Tantrik art as a "mega-person": Tantrik yoga is moreover directed to reversing the process by assembling and, as it were, neutralizing the numerous forms created by *māya*, including Time, re-enacting the union of the cosmic dyad with a human sáktī, and finally reassembling the original monad via a sexually induced oceanic experience. Certainly there is a sense in which "the world" as we perceive it is created through our own process of individuation, and this, not galaxy formation, is what Tantrik philosophy is talking about. To treat it as erroneous or mythical objective cosmology is merely naive: more interesting, perhaps, to a scientific–empirical culture is the fact that Tantrik exploration of inner space is based on at least as much experimentation, and almost as elaborate a technology, as objective astronomy—only it is psychotechnology expressed in yantras, rituals and an elaborate series of body image manipulations. We may be intellectually more receptive to this store of experimental evidence as we attempt to explore the nature of I-ness from scratch.

The extension of this self-exploration to a mysticized cosmology in the macrocosm seems a natural consequence of the attempt to experience I–That fusion and nondifference. We might be more inclined to follow Śaṅkara and re-examine how much the structure of our own mental processes has influenced the structure we attribute to external events—the Tantrik might argue that it clearly does so, if only in our objectification of observing "selves." Science is a device intended to circumvent our capacity for sympathetic magic, and to facilitate the assumption that microcosm and macrocosm have to be similarly patterned: it makes possible the avoidance of anthropocentric cosmologies centering in man, or in Mount Meru, which are projected mandalas identifying the general universe with our perception of self. We now seem about ready to deal with the problems of objective versus subjective experience in both modes at once, or to put it differently, we now have the equipment to look objectively at the subjective and inner-space experiences of the Tantriks, and to appreciate the biases in the equipment with which "we" perform objective studies. This is not an undertaking in which science can "lose out" to woolly intuitivism—it has taken systems theory and neurology to indicate to the West that the ancient sadhus were describing real experiences, not arbitrary flights of imagination. On the other hand, the dissolution of the I, which exists by virtue of cogitating, into a virtual or illusory brain experience is bound to blur a little the boundary between in and out, between objective and subjective. The consequences are bound to be novel, and to create in both philosophy and science a rather different style from that of the nineteenth century, which more than any other fortified the primacy of I-ness as the most important human experience. It will be interesting to see what happens when two brands of empiricism—the objectivist empiricism of science and the introspective empiricism of the "mystic"—combine. Perhaps the combination may begin in fields where square objectivism already leads to paradoxical results—subatomic physics and the interpretation of time are cases in point.

VII.3
Individuative cosmologies— Tantrik

In the individuative cosmology of Tantric Hinduism, there is an original monad composed of two potential parts, a "male" (immanent or intellectual) principle and a "female" principle (śaktī) which corresponds to "activity" or "energy." The monad consists of their fusion in coition—directed, like the ritual coition which Tantric adepts practice to recapture the primal state, to "bliss" rather than to creation or reproduction. At some stage the two components of the monad become aware of their separate potentials. The śaktī opens her eyes, disengages herself from the male principle and engages in a dance which generates *maya*, or divisive illusion. Whereas the experience of the monad was oceanic and un-differentiated, the creative dance of the female principle causes the male principle, which observes it, to perceive reality as divided into categories, objects and states, and time as a serial reality rather than as a simultaneity. It is the viewing of the activity of the female, pattern-forming, principle by the male, logical, principle which dissipates the oceanic perception of one-ness. To recreate the original one-ness and dissipate the illusion of seriality and diversity, the Tantric yogi re-enacts the stages described in the model, engaging in ritual intercourse with a consecrated human partner and magnifying the fusional experience of sexuality into a fusional experience involving all perceptions. In Tantric Buddhism the sexes of the polar principles are reversed, the male being Energy and the female Immanence, but the rationale of resynthesis is the same.

The use of sexuality as a tool in achieving the removal of categories is the chief peculiarity of the Tantric tradition. In conventional Hinduism the subdivision of Brahman without-qualities into Brahman with-qualities, and human experience from unitary to a multiplicity of illusory divisions proceeds in the same way, but the resynthesis is achieved internally, by awakening a concealed or sleeping female energy residing in the genitals (*kundalinī*—the curled one) and directing it upward along an imaginary series of centers visualized as existing in the spine: the familiar inner-technology of meditative or solitary yoga.

In one particularly interesting version, the śaktī is represented as creating diversity of perception by "holding a mirror" to the "light" or unitary image of the male-discursive principle, reflecting that light on "the wall which is consciousness." This description (in the *Kāmakalāvilāsa*) is the closest Hindu parallel to the explicit idea of identity = experience of diversity = a reflection, or time-delay process which we suggested as a systems model of I-ness, and is of particular interest because it must have been derived wholly by introspection, in the course of experiment with manipulated oceanic states.

The Śankhya Tattva diagrams given by Rawson (p. 115) illustrate the structure of "cosmic individuation" as interpreted by Tantric Hinduism. They are originally intended to derive a kind of inner-cosmology of individuation from the process of resynthesis of nondifference aimed at by Tantric yoga. It is interesting, however, that they closely parallel the kind of history which we have attributed to the sensation of identity. From an initial state of nondifference, a gestalt perception (corresponding here to the śaktī) and a verbal-logical ("male") perception differentiate, and one of these, by way of an ongoing *déjà vu*, monitors the other: in the Indian model this corresponds to the "opening of the eyes" of the śaktī. As a result of this division, the female principle generates māya, the illusion of different objects and categories. This, however, is another way of saying that categorization is a product of identity-sense, which experiences difference and draws the distinction of self and other. Assuming that it is the discursive mode which is the slower, and monitors the nondiscursive, this fits better with the Buddhist Tantrik model of the "female" component as passive (*śunya*) and the male or discursive having its eyes open and doing the creation, but in either event it looks as if yogic mystics, in charting the method by which they contrive to abolish I-ness as against That-ness, give a plausibly translatable version of the manner in which the sense of identity appears in individual ontogeny. Even the identification of "female" properties with the nondominant hemisphere is echoed in the Tantrik use of "left-" and "right-hand" worship.

The exact nature of the Tantrik manipulation of sexual experience is difficult to extract from the written literature and complicated by accessory beliefs such as the conservation of semen.

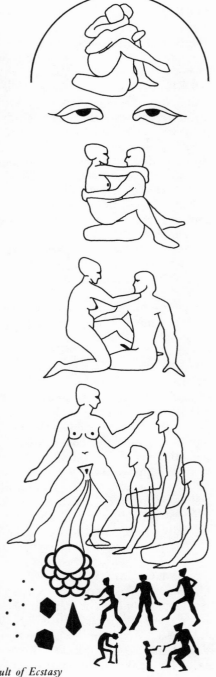

The all-embracing whole of Reality

Reality divided as the sexual pair, Shiva and Shakti, within both man and world, so deeply joined they are unaware of their differences and beyond Time

The sexual pair become aware of their distinction

The female "objective" separates from the male "subject"

The female "objective" performs Her dance of illusion, persuading the male "subject" he is not one but many, and generating from Her womb the world of multiplied objects in what seems to be a sequence in time

"Subjects" perceive a differentiated reality, seeming to be composed of separate particles of objective fact, and live lives that seem to be extended in time

From: Rawson, *Tantra, the Indian Cult of Ecstasy*

The success of the operation depends by tradition on the female partner (śaktī, ḍakinī) who is the initiatrix. The most highly dramatized experiences were held to occur in a burning-ground (as a reminder of self-dissolution and a rejection of caste barriers, which such a setting would pollute) and during a menstrual period. These symbolic adjuncts apart, the process of reconstituting the monad, in which through nondifference each partner "becomes" the other, begins by concentration on the genitalia as community property. One such step is for the śaktī to visualize an "internal" penis with which she penetrates the urethra of her male partner; another is to attempt to experience the genitalia as transposed (the lingam is hers, the yonī his; this transposition is depicted in some Tibetan ikons). Arousal is then used to generalize this transposition into an experienced fusion of body images, so that each partner becomes subjectively both God and Goddess, and then to extend this acategorical experience of self so that it includes all other objects, and becomes oceanic. How, beyond this schema, the ḍakinī facilitates these perceptive modifications has not been intelligibly described—one would expect verbal suggestion coupled with muscular control, touch (nyāsa) and the use of stylized mystical sounds (mantra) common to all Tantric psychomanipulations. It would require to be experienced to be comprehended. A proper record of the traditional rite might throw a lot of light on the sexual and individuative components of the body image.

The transformation of sexual into religious experience in the Hindu left-hand tradition begins with taboo-breaking and sexual koininia heightened by ritual, expectation, and the prior consumption of vijaya (cannabis). The critical feature of the ritual intercourse, from the physiological viewpoint, is that in it breath-control is combined with control of emission (whether this finally takes places, as in Hindu ritual, or is suppressed altogether, as in Buddhist) so as to produce suppression of I-ness. Breath-control is a familiar feature of hatha-yoga generally—applying it in intercourse is a popular recipe against premature ejaculation in secular practice, but it also has the effect of actively resisting the physiological overbreathing which normally accompanies sexual excitement. The aim of the instructed Tantrik couple is both to control this and to reach the verge of orgasm, and then to arrest the process at this point, and it is this double arrest which is the launching-pad for the fusional experience. The effect of this combined exercise is perhaps to induce anoxia (or hypercapnia) and to combine the physiological effects of this with the suppression of external impressions, the alteration of consciousness, and the fusional experiences which normally occur in pre-orgasm, making the combination last. In this context the postponement of ejaculation makes sense apart from Indian ejaculatory mythology— it aims to prolong an exceptional state of mind and use it, rather as astronomers use an eclipse of the Sun, for experimentation not possible under other conditions. In ordinary, nonritual sex, the "window" is of too short a duration for any but a transient experience of oceanic perception, since it is overtaken by orgasm and detumescence.

The form of the experience is patterned partly by physiology and partly by ideology and expectation. In theory the hierogamy—the union of Śiva with Śaktī, from which arise both phenomenal reality and time—is a figure for the development of the self-monitoring process: māya, the creative "illusion" through which the perceived world subsists, is not so much illusion as the individuative and objectivizing viewpoint. And the yogic undertaking is to get behind māya by retracing individuation, refusing Śiva with Śaktī, and perceive experientially that both objective "reality" and linear time are conditional, or optional, ways of experiencing the not-I. To take another culturally distinct image which we explored in looking at the neurology of identity "reality" to the Hindu religious empiric is like a hologram, consisting of an infinite array of wave-fronts, and māya the effect whereby, when this array is scanned by the objectivizing human brain from the viewpoint of objective identity, the illusion of solid objects appears. Turn off the "laser," and the hologram is again a mass of resonances and periodicities of which the observer is now a part, nondifferent from the entire pattern, and containing it in microcosm, as holograms contain all of the elicitable information in all of their parts. Creation is not seen as evolution or process, the objectivizing view, but as a function of the human viewpoint as it elicits pattern from an array.

The outside of a Śaiva temple is covered with figuration—the developed hologram. The inside commonly contains only the emblem of the union between Immanence and Activity, the cosmic counterparts of the Gestalt and the verbal–logical modes of perception: indeed, the female–active principle, generatrix of maya, is also explicitly identified with speech (*Vāc*). Hinduism in its wide variety and antiquity has, of course, enormously elaborated this model, as theology, philosophy and poetry, as well as in ritual and dogma, but the underlying discovery remains common—that the intuitive view of what is "objective," including time-as-sequence, is a conditional view, that its conditionality can be experienced, and that this experience is to be had by way of an operation on the sense of I-ness, the induced oceanic experience.

VII.4
Individuative cosmologies— the Kabbalah

Hindu ideas in this field are derived from looking in, not from looking out.

It is interesting that despite the militant monism of the Jewish tradition, and its firm conception of God as Other, the Kabbalah echoes similar concerns. God himself is the Great Face (*mahāpuruṣa*) from whom emanate *sefiroth* or *murtīs*. Not only do these include a transcendent man, the probable progenitor of Blake's Giant Albion (Adam Kadmon, Adam Elo-oh), but according to Simeon ben-Yohai:

> "The form of Man contains all that is in heaven above and upon earth below, the superior as well as the inferior beings . . . the human form contains all things, and all that is exists only by virtue of it."[47]

Moreover in the process of creation, the emanations of the One God acquire opposite sexual polarity, active and passive, male and female, King and Queen, Beauty and *Shekinah* (immanence)—"all that exists, all that has been formed by the Ancient (Whose name be sanctified) can exist only in a male and a female [form]." Similarly the various *sefiroth* govern various parts of the body image and can be used to manipulate it. Even the Indivisible One is *trimurtī* (threefold in manifestation), possessing "three heads sculptured one in another and one above another," these being hidden wisdom, which is never unveiled; above that, the Ancient; and above that "a head which is not a head" and is qualityless, being called No Thing (*Ayn*), in Sanskrit *Iśvara nirguna*.

It is dangerous to infer that this kind of system creation is the result of introspection by Jewish mystics—it could equally have come through the Judaizing of non-Judaic mystical literature—but despite its rejection by orthodoxy its influence has been considerable, chiefly among non-Jewish religious speculators like Blake and Agrippa who raided it for formulations in preference to the more coherent, but less culturally acceptable, corpus of Hindu philosophy, and also in Jewish popular religious tradition. One interesting feature of the kabbalah is the graphic vision of Deity as the "vast Face," complete with brain, hair and skull, and of an intense brightness, which generates objective Nature by emanation. At one level, this vision is pantheistic—the objective world has a face, it is person-like and can be addressed. At another, God, who is both the soul and intellect of the world and at the same time transcendent, is seen as having created large numbers of past worlds, symbolized by the "Kings of Edom," which were abortive because he was unable to establish relationship with them: to the authors of the *Zohar* these hypothetical worlds were created as perishable self-contained systems like soap-bubbles, which drifted off and burst. It is only with the creation of Man, Adam Elo-oh, that the "Great Face" is provided with a chariot (Merkaba) in which to descend *into* creation—Man in this image is the vehicle by which creative intelligence is objectivized in the Universe. The kabbalah seems here to express the tension between intuitive experience that the perception of structure in the universe is within, and the powerful Judaic objectivization of God as other, as not-I, which modern scientism transfers to the objective cosmos; the uneasiness to which Zaehner refers when objectivizing religions find it necessary to confront oceanic experiences which suggest that the "Great Face" is a reflection of our own—of our body image, in fact, in one of its extensions.

VII.5
Individuative cosmologies—
Blake

William Blake was indeed almost alone among western explorers of the intuitive structure of mind, both in the richness of his interpretation, and in the clarity with which he seems to have perceived what he was doing. For Blake, "Four Great Ones are in every Man" namely the four Spiritual Senses of the Blakeian pleroma: passion, sensation, intellect and imagination; but these beings, while having quasi-personal attributes, are together with their śaktīs, specters (negatives) and emanations (anima-figures) quite unequivocally internal, and their field of operation is the human nervous system: "All Deities reside within the human breast" and, more explicitly, "In the Brain of Man we live & in his circling Nerves, this bright world of all our joy is in the Human Brain," says Enitharmon (Space) to Los (Time, Prophecy, Imagination).

The importance of Blake as a philosopher and psychologist has been overshadowed by his artistic performance. It is strange that unlike Swedenborg he never became the originator of a religious cult, for the religion he states is singularly apt to modern knowledge. As to macrocosm and microcosm, the world "is" flat, not spheroidal, to anyone except an astronaut: on a long voyage, or in building a freeway, it "becomes" curved. "There is an Outside spread Without & an Outside spread Within," and accordingly phenomenology is structured by the structure of human perception, the objective being that which is perceived as not-self and reasonably consistent in its manifestation. This strikingly modern philosophical position, buried as it is in Blake's highly poetic rewriting of *Paradise Lost* as he considered that a Milton liberated from conventional Puritanism would have written it, has not been sufficiently recognized for what it is.

Blake's complete system is too complex to describe in detail here—it includes, for example, the idea that Good and Evil are not the attributes of persons but of "states": Satan is a "state" of logical perception (Urizen) not an inherently evil or hubristic force. Unlike the Tantric model, Blake's system is a cosmology, not a cosmogony. It has no special interest in individuation, and is concerned not with oceanic experience as an enlightening goal but with a comprehensive intellect which simply takes oceanic perception for granted, and its absence, as a complement of reason, mere evidence of blindness— the result and the cause of falling into māyā ("Ulro" in Blake's terminology), the web of illusion produced by unintelligent and unimaginative literalism. There is no pattern of stages—the time-scale of all this is taken as tjukurpa, not even as nominally sequential, and in the symbolism the same persons alternate as one another's parents, lovers and progeny in a timeless complex of interrelation. Intellect, in Blake's terminology, represents *sahāja*, the ongoing awareness of logical and oceanic modes of perception as natural alternatives, a way of normal life rather than a succession of glimpses attained by spiritual exercise.

The key model of Blake's system is expressed in his illustration to the poem "Milton," which shows Man enclosed in the shell of objective reality, and situated at the intersection of the realms of Intellect, Passion, Sensation and Imagination. The four "Great Ones"—Urizen, Reason, Luvah, Passion, Tharmas, Sensation, and Los (Urthona), Time and Imagination, overlap within the "mundane egg," the envelope of human experience. Enlightenment, or Intellect, consists of the equipoise of all four, in contrast to the Urizenian preoccupation with rules, technology, and the literal. In "Adam," until he is seduced by linear reason to start making ethical rules for himself, Imagination predominates over literalism. In "Satan," literalism and legalism, the specter or perversion of Urizen ("he who limits") predominate over creative Imagination. Blake's

THE BLAKEIAN PLEROMA

(Based on Northrop Frye, Fearful Symmetry, with minor alterations)

MAN (Albion) and his ANIMA (Jerusalem)

contain

	LUVAH	URIZEN	THARMAS	URTHONA
Eternal Name	(Passion)	(Reason)	(Sensation)	(Imagination)
Earthly Name	Orc	Satan	Covering Cherub	Los
	(Revolution)	(Opacity)	(Self-hood)	(Creativity)
Bride (Śaktī)	Vala (Nature)	Ahania (Nirvana)	Enion (Generation)	Enitharmon (Spirituality)
Quality	Passion	Logic	Fusion	Prophecy
Negative	Hate	Doubt	Despair	Dulness
Beast	Bull	Lion	Eagle	Man
Ćakra	Genitals	Head	Heart	Spirit-self
Symbol	Stars	Sun	Moon	Mountain
State	Generation ("nature")	Eden (Good and evil)	Beulah (pre-Edipal bliss)	Ulro (māya)
Son of Los	Palambron (pity)	Rintrah (wrath)	Theotormon (jealousy)	Bromion (terror)
Son's śaktī	Elynittria	Ocalythron	Oothoon	none
Occupation	Weaver	Plowman	Shepherd	Smith

"Four Mighty Ones are in every Man; a Perfect Unity
Cannot exist but from the Universal Brotherhood of Eden,
The Universal Man, to Whom be Glory Evermore."

In Blake's "mystical" poems the four Zoas ("living things") with their śaktis, offspring and emanations constitute the "mental fauna" of Man. Roughly speaking, the God of conventional religion ("Nobodaddy") is a manifestation of Satan/Urizen or legalism. The function of Christ, identified by Blake sometimes with Luvah (passion, revolution) and sometimes with Los (poetic imagination), is to achieve unison of the Four which collapses their destructive separation and ends the division of animus and anima which is dramatized in the division of the sexes. The aim of this yoga is not separate oceanic experience so much as a constant ability to exist in both the objective and the subjective world, Blake's definition of "intellect." While the very rough outline above helps the reader to make sense of the poems it does not do justice to the complexity of Blake's vision. It helps to keep in mind that the "four Beasts" are *forces in the human mind*, not external deities. Blake divides all human perceptions and activities between them—thus Los and Enitharmon also represent the human perceptions of Time and of Space respectively.

assault on legalistic religion, hellbent interventionist technologism, and the religion of objectivity, as exemplified in early nineteenth-century rationalism and the Industrial Revolution, focuses on the imbalance of Reason and Imagination, rather than on the roles of the other two Zoas: Sensuality has been banished by legalism and guilt—Passion is a creative or a disruptive force according to whether Los or Urizen predominates. Each of the Great Ones is endowed with a śaktī—the God of conventional religions; "Nobodaddy," a perversion of Urizen-Satan, is the God of this world. Milton, the type of the prophetic poet forced to wrestle with an objectivist and legalist culture, has to force his way through the realm of Urizen (his Puritan theology) to penetrate the Veil of Illusion and regain the oceanic-rational vision for himself and for man. He is assisted in this undertaking by his anima Ololon, a feminine principle to whom acategorical and undogmatic vision comes naturally, and whom Milton, as a result of his cultural setting, has expelled from his "self," thus diminishing his own capacity for total experience.

The whole Blakeian pleroma, necessary for an understanding of the elaborate fourfold maṇḍala structure underlying the poems, is set out on p. 121, based on the interpretation of the Blakeian scholar Northrop Frye. We need not bother here with its detailed structure—Blake speaks most directly to us through the vision of wholeness which he expresses in a magnificent synthesis of poetry and visual art. Where he differs from Tantrik, and all previous, inner travellers is in his firm assumption of the complete naturalness of "fourfold vision," in which reason, the "religion" of his culture, is qualified by feeling, sensuality and oceanic imagination as a matter of course.

Whereas in Tantrik yoga the use of unconventional sexuality is dependent in part on the shock-value of taboo-breaking, Blake takes the more modern view that sexual openness, not taboo-breaking, is a facilitator and a natural consequence of personal completeness, and requires no sacred context provided that the heart be right. Jealousy, and the interpretation of love as something which "drinks another as a sponge drinks water" is an archetypal work of the devil, implying the Urizenic ownership of one person by another. This idea, the subject of the "Song of the Daughters of Albion," and of the poem-section appearing in Blake's engraving above the diagram of Milton's journey, harks back to the literal Milton's marital problems and the production of his *Tetrachordon*, but Blake seizes on it as a test of good faith, and a sacramental use of sexuality in general.

Although prophecy depends on vision, not prevision, it is hard not to see Blake—who was regarded in his time as a competent but eccentric minor artist—as a cultural innovator of giant stature who arrived at an insight into the style of a period one epoch ahead of his own time. The vast symbolism in which he expressed the world-view of that style was partly protective—set out in the language of the religion of objectivity it would have led to his confinement. It has taken the playing-out of moralism, objectivism and the era of Urizen to bring us to a point where we see what he is talking about. Although we are unlikely to adopt his symbolism, Blake is expounding the religion of the twenty-first century out of the context of the nineteenth—a remarkable imaginative feat.

VII.6
Individuative cosmologies—conclusion

Cosmologies, in that they are all saturated with the body image experience of the cosmologist, are in terms of our argument by nature religious (this includes scientific cosmologies, since a definition of religion in terms of delimitation of the I for purposes of fixing what we will term "That" would make science, semantically at least, a "religion"). The microcosm or body so projected is the "subtle body," or the clutch of body image experiences which repeatedly surface under introspection—mandalas, tree-of-life symbols, mazes like the Manas Ćakra of the Tantriks (which, as Argüelles points out, even looks a little like a brain).[48] Other of these experiences influence cosmology only at a remove—the whole yogic routine of ascending ćakras and the Brahma-opening, called by the Hopi the "door in the top of the head"[49] are of this type. Given the fact that under zoistic conditions neither education nor society produce the effort of will necessary to keep the I firmly objectivized and objectivizing and thought linear, these are probably very early human discoveries, together with the knacks of bringing them to experience, ranging from dancing and drumming to the eating of magic mushrooms. When attention is focused on them, they are recognized as body–I experiences. When it is not, they remain "archetypal" and bob up in cosmologies, as the alchemists started to study what we call chemistry and ended with an elaborate exploration of what we call Jungian psychology, or a complex combination of the two. Shut the door, and they come in the windows. Science has the problem of keeping such interiora out, but depends on them for models; and has not really yet addressed the $64,000 question, how far they have nonetheless got in, and must get in, to any statement we make about the external because they are a part of the system which is doing the perceiving.

VII.7
The intuition of cyclicity

Gnostic and similar theogonies, as I have pointed out, are the result of introspection about human individuation and the way in which the structure of that process "creates" the objective world—it is a fundamental error, due to our religious assumptions as scientific objectivists, which make us treat them as simply erroneous and arbitrary cosmologies: we are looking at the wrong cosmos.

Another intuitive pattern derived from introspection which is widespread in religion-making is that of cyclicity, exemplified in the pre-Columbian calendars and the Hindu yugas. This is equally meaningless to modern, and particularly Christian, ontology, since the counterpart of objectivist abstraction *vis-à-vis* "reality" is linear historicism. Cyclical intuitions, in spite of modern mystics who try to use them as some evangelicals use Biblical prophecy, are not accounts of objective history.

It is reasonably easy, once their nature has been pointed out, to see how Hindu and Gnostic theogonies correspond to the intuition of the way in which the individual in development, and man in history, have "created" an objective world through the peculiarities and structure of the identity experience, and those who have mystical and oceanic experiences can verify the intuitive model by re-collapsing the structures we normally perceive as objective into the alternative, primal or nirvikalpa mode of experience. It is a good deal harder, however, to make much discursive sense of the conviction of cyclicity. Probably the important thing to realize in attempting to see what mental structures this view represents is that the linear view of history, imposed not only by our awareness of evolution and our conviction of progress, but by the accuracy of our records, is a counter-intuitive one. Myths do not have a historical timescale. The idea expressed linguistically by native Australians that there are two temporal categories, "now" and "not-now," tjukurpa, which also implies "holy" or "mythical," is general in mythology. Christianity has militated against this view, and in favour of objective historicism, by focusing on a single event, the life and death of Christ: nevertheless in his tjukurpa significance, even a historical Christ is perpetually resacrificed in the Mass and perpetually recrucified and re-resurrected at Easter. Myths, in other words, are not real-time sequences but ongoing truths objectified; both our injection of literal historicism into Christianity and our treatment of non-Christian myths as false historical beliefs are the results of a humanly unusual view of time. Our civilization is the first one able, through palaeontology and archaeology, to give an objective account of past events in their real-time sequence, but this is recent. Only a century ago Bishop Usher's biblical chronology still had adherents. In fact an objective ordering of real-time events on a basis of evidence is a cultural result of the assumption of linearity, not its cause. We set out to objectivize history because we had come to abandon the older intuitive position that "all is always Now," at least insofar as long-term processes are concerned.

I have suggested that the linear perception of Time as a one-way sequence is a product of the process by which we objectivize Identity. Whatever cultural process has led us to objectivize That has also led us to objectivize Then.

In preliterate societies the now/tjukurpa division of time, even if not linguistically explicit, is adequate and often implied. There is an awareness of short-run history, but its accuracy fades with the natural attrition of eyewitnesses—anything which the oldest surviving person did not witness is already merged with tradition and colored by the mythical. Popular historical conceptions still behave in this way—names persist over very long periods, but actual events undergo mythical agglomeration and attrition: thus Robin Hood assembled the deeds of a great many outlaws, took over the ballad sagas of Adam Bell, Clym of the Clough, and other personages, many of whom were historical, and ended as a symbolic figure similar to Hercules. The horizon within which real-time history closes down into archetypal tradition has rarely been large and, even in the presence of record, intuitive and mythopoetic "history" is always inclined to take over: the interpretation of Roman history by the Jacobins or of the American Revolution by generations of Americans owe as much to archetypes as to fact.

Civilizations with cyclical intuitions built into their world view, such as the pre-Columbian Mexicans and the Hindus, encountered practical difficulties over their relevance to linear events—the Spanish conquest of Mexico was facilitated by its coincidence with the cyclical calendar which led the Aztecs to expect a theophany. This sort of categorical confusion must have begun early, at or before the time when Stonehenge was constructed, in that archetypal astrology cannot fail under its own impetus to turn into real-time astronomy. The mental intuitions of cyclicity, analogous to the spatial intuition of the mandala, which arise from introspection of inner structure must have seemed to early man excitingly consonant with the long-term cycles observed in the movements of heavenly bodies. Having acquired a schematic principle, however, and particularly when that principle carries the conviction derived from introspection, there is no problem in finding literal events to which it can be applied: the Hindu yugas do in fact coincide plausibly with human cultural history, even though at the literal level there is abundant evidence that only one such sequence has in fact occurred.

Just as the tjukurpa interpretation of celestial cyclicity provided an exciting fit with the observation of literal cyclicity, the inner-world conviction of cyclicity which so excited William Yeats in his wife's visions and the writings of Michael Robartes can be applied with plausible results to the observed process of relaxation-oscillation in cultural styles, the replacement of intuitivist by objectivist perception characteristic of the rise of the West, and the revaluation of the intuitive which seems to represent the next forthcoming change in cultural style. What we see here, however, is not a mystical insight into the future (the same prevision could be given on wholly rationalist grounds today) but the exact analogy of the way in which the objective experience which we have of categories is patterned by the structure of the mind which does the experiencing. The popularity of the conviction of an impending change of style and the birth of a "rough beast" representing such a change naturally rises at times when a world view has become dys-homeostatic, as the technological–objective view of "progress" has now become, and as the flaccid quietism of the Middle Ages became in the Renaissance. A prophet, after all, is not someone with a magical ability to foresee real-time events, but someone with an explicit perception of human mental structures which most of us, though governed by the same structures in our thinking, do not share. It does not now require a prophet to see the inherent limitations of literalism and objectivism, or to predict that insightless technology will prove unliveable: at the time that William Blake was writing, however, it did require one, because the whole direction of cultural style was dictated by enthusiasm for a *progressisme* which experience—and, incidentally, a broader development of science itself—have punctured.

What was strikingly prophetic about Blake's view, however, was not that he saw industrialism as the counterpart of a Tibetan Bardo state analogous to hell, but that he recognized the complementarity of intuitive and objective experience—most mystical intuitivists are pessimists who see no good in anything except intuition, rather as most objective literalists see the reservations of mystics about human mental patterning as nonsenses which can be defused by objective demonstration. Although for a prophetic view the future is pre-dictable because "all is always now," and Blakeian intellect has always consisted of a balance between intuitive and logical perceptions, cyclicity in history is not truly cyclical—the process we see is spiral, in that the re-fusion of logical–objective with inner-perceptive ontogenies will now be effected through, not in spite of, the appreciation of structure which we have derived from abandoning crude intuitivism. So far from being enemies, the Four Great Ones, including both Prophetic Imagination and Discursive Science, are indispensable allies in the creation of a holistic philosophy, and demonic only when, under the impulsion of cultural blindness or psychopathology, they "go it alone." It is our commitment to empirical science which now makes a revolution in cultural style towards a revaluation of introspection inevitable.

What if anything the intuition of cyclicity represents in terms of introspection is harder to define. Most probably it arises from the intuition of circularity and symmetry which reflect our perception of I-ness as being "central," the one-way perception of time which is inherent in the homuncular *déjà-vu*, and commonsense experience of repetition and recurrence in the objective world. It is interesting that in oceanic experience, when directional as well as categorical classification is suspended, the intuition of cycle becomes prominent. The measurement of time is probably itself a function of self-regarding identity, and perceptual processes in the brain may well involve elements of scan: under these conditions cerebral cyclicity may well be perceived *sub specie aeternitatis*, and produce the intuition of cyclicity, rather as cerebral symmetry and visual projection produce the intuition of symmetry–free–running projections of two of our most important processes of pattern-perception, through which the categories of normal, I-centered perception are transduced.

Be that as it may, the objectivist man, endowed with a discrete and self-regarding I-ness combined with an equally self-regarding Now-ness, while he has always represented one modality of human self-experience, is a contingent being. One part of the activity of religions has been the exploration and qualification of this view through introspection which leads to other potential experiences both of identity and of temporality.

VIII.1
"Ethical" religion

Besides the objectification of disembodied intelligences and powers, old-time religion-defining has attached weight to the idea that "religion" as opposed to magic and sorcery is a higher class of goods, involving salutary awe from which springs ethical obligation. This is to my mind a bent view of religion in origin, but true in a sense not intended by its postulators. Ethics do arise from the defining of Self, because they deal with interaction with other Selves: not in this case parts of our own inner experience seen, as it were, out of the tail of our inner eye, but objective Others with whom we relate, on whom we project our own experiences, and whose experiences we introject. The point about this mechanism is that it is both evolved and adaptive in social animals even at the lowest probable level of discursive self-experience—most birds will run risks in defense of young or of conspecifics, and such ethics, though not motivated by philosophy, are biologically indistinguishable from the human version.

Human ethics really repose not so much in religions as in cultures, of which religions are of course a part. "Religions" have pretended to ethical expertise in a distinct field, however: while cultures lay down what not to do for fear of offending our neighbors, they lay down what not to do lest we offend the nonhuman. This kind of instruction is in its origins less ethics than public health—if the eating of kangaroos offends the kangaroo spirit and drives away game, that is a consideration as practical as the belief that handling plutonium offends the plutonium spirit and is dangerous to our health. This activity is better termed rule-making, and since it tends to follow Parkinson's law, the spiritual, as opposed to the religious, have from the Gnostics to Blake attributed it not to a God but to a pseudo-God, the projected matter of everything Kant was told before the age of five, in other words, Nobodaddy. It is a fantastic state, anthropologically, that we have reached when since the middle of the last century ethicists have seriously argued that without belief in a legislating deity morality loses all rational sanction and must founder.

VIII.2
Good, evil and bliss

It is easy, though not strictly fair, to attribute the Christian orthodox suspicion of yogic-type mysticisms to the dislike of ecclesiastical authorities for do-it-yourself religious experience. An equally powerful factor can be seen if we compare St Francis of Assisi with Ramakrishna. Francis had most of the attributes of a sadhu but not the elitism which makes Hindu sages concentrate singlemindedly on enlightenment. Both he and they embrace poverty, but Francis had before him the specific injunctions of Christ that enlightenment involved feeding the hungry, healing the sick and identifying with the poor—operations which traditional yoga in *ārya-dharma* would see, and not from uncompassion, as irrelevant to the true aim of knowing Brahman. This part of Christian mysticism, that samadhi involves ethical activity, poses problems: if the evils we are enjoined to remedy, and which caused Christ to be crucified, are not māya, or even karma, who put them there? God? Man? The devil? Concentration on identity-based experience is easier for a sadhu who does not see the Problem of Evil as a problem—Christian sages inevitably do so, and the very existence of that problem opens the road back into formulations which are those which Freud uncovered and humans acquire from childhood experience, the superego formulations, legalism, atonement, the rule of Urizen, and many of the contortions of early heresiology. Yet to ignore suffering and fix the mind on Brahman, while it may reflect the rejection of "inferior benevolence," strikes us as lacking in a religious vitamin.

Christian mysticism also contributes a unique religious note in a "sense of sin," arising from its awareness of evil, which is truly philosophical at its best, and neither ritual nor simply irrational, like the prohibitions of Urizen. True, its phylogeny includes ritual sins, like those prescribed in Judaic law, which are typical of legislating religions, and both in orthodoxy and in private opinion sins have been Freudianized into antisexuality and masochistic behaviors—it is hard not to find the unworthiness-feelings of so great a mystic as St Teresa embarrassing and at variance with her good sense. But no amount of populist hellfire (which also occurs in vulgar Hinduism) or of irrational antihedonism can entirely overrule the genuine and essential contribution of sin, of flawedness in creation, to Christian mysticism. A synthesis which gets rid of this by attributing it to Illusion—once we see Brahman, evil and good make sense because they no longer appear relevant—is easier to take, but it is sidestepping something: Christian mysticism is bound to be concerned with the issue of where in the I the flaw occurs, whether it is no more fundamental than an unfortunate consequence of the software of childhood experience, whether it has a cosmological or Manichean extension, and so on. When such a mystic experiences samādhi, one of its main attractions is that Brahman is experienced as flawless—at the dvaita stage the contrast may be unbearable, as it was for Gerontius, but once merged with the "goodness of God" the tension is extinguished in redemption, graphically described by a writer so little like a traditional mystic as John Bunyan. This is a component of religion strikingly characteristic of Christianity, which we should not allow vulgarized or reaction-formation versions to obscure.

The extent to which this conviction of flawedness is an offshoot of the experience of I-ness, and of the uneasiness of incorporation of superego experiences into it which leaves both the "great Man" and the shadow self as partially outside I would be worth re-examining. Quite possibly what Adam learned from the apple was less the knowledge of Good and Evil than the sense of the Self, with consequent suspension, except for brief recoveries under the influence of intense spiritual exercise, of a perpetual samādhi. Practicing mystics point out that too little emphasis has been put on the fact that samādhi is blissful—one million times the bliss of Indra, says the text—or, in other words, highly reinforcing. Now "bliss" and similar designations are very nearly the fingerprints of what we should term pre-Edipal recreations, states of mind *before* the consolidation of homuncular I-ness, *before* the switching-on of troublesome early psychosexual reactions, *before* the attempt to introject a superego; the contrast is between flawed and unflawed, with a certain antinomian character about it which charismatic and sexually ecstatic social rituals attempt to recreate by enactment, and the cataclysmal oceanic experience recreates by I-suppression. This is in line with the idea that samādhi is not the turning-on of some kind of spiritual awareness so much as the turning-off of a learned set of self-experience which has been incorporated during development into our neurology but which can be, or become, reversed, either spontaneously or by means of appropriate maneuvers. If so, that the conviction of sin should have led some Christians—including nontheological folk like John Bunyan—to become mystics, and to term samādhi salvation, is unsurprising, and puts the sin-and-redemption emphasis in Christian thinking back into the general stream of religion-making.

Good, evil, and abstractions therefrom, while they are of obvious practical importance to a social animal programmed to a dialogue between I and Thou, and the "knowledge" which Adam acquired from the apple, do however belong to a different "layer" of experience from those I am here classifying as religious, deeply as Christian belief and Christian humanism, or concern, have involved the two. Dean Inge once wrote that

> "the illumination of the mystic has strictly speaking no moral side; for morality, in the ordinary sense, is left behind. As the anonymous French mystic who wrote *The Mirror of Simple Souls* puts it: 'Virtues, I take leave of you. Once I was your servant, now I am delivered from your thralldom.' What he means is that in the higher stage morality has become autonomous and spontaneous . . . God's service has become perfect freedom."[50]

Or rather, as Meister Eckhart said "there, neither vice nor virtue ever entered in." Ethics, after all, are a function of dialog, and totally fusional religious experiences would seem to exclude them, there being nobody left to whom one can do good or ill. I am not here attempting to exhaust the relation between religions and ethics, or the legitimacy of philosophical concern with a problem of evil—but the "existential" view that in the kernel of religion authenticity ("good faith") in regard to the experience of identity is the only surviving value seems to have something in its favor. It is interesting that neither Christian salvation or samādhi are offered as making humans infallibly virtuous—one offers atonement and the other enlightenment, but the practical effects are only, at the ethical level, to elevate behavior to what is acceptable for the culture and capable of emulation by unredeemed or unenlightened people of good ethical sense—the *religious* effects of these processes are quite other.

The leading moral hazard of formal religion appears to be righteous bigotry: one genuine hazard of total focus upon oceanic or other unusual experiences is a virulent form of élitist antinomianism. The next commonest prescription for mystical experience after rigid askesis is the solemn rejection of taboos—a very ancient technique of the shaman, who reverses all customary priorities. In its laudable form this implies simply total dedication to project and novelty of vision—the equivalent of Dubedat's artistic creed; in a less laudable form it can degenerate into demonism, rather as Tantrik worship has occasionally degenerated into sorcery—Kapalika yogis of the tenth century were reputed to engage in human sacrifice out of love of the Goddess and zeal to obtain occult powers, whereas European Christians continued to practice it into the seventeenth century and beyond out of hatred for heretics. The moral is probably only that corrupt and disturbed people will behave in character, and in so doing may create social sanction for cruelty and anomie. Formal religions, like political ideologies, have accordingly tended, when they were inhuman, to institutionalize inhumanity. By contrast the experimental mystic must be occupationally oblivious of common convention and is highly reinforced in being so. As there is nothing in the oceanic experience *per se* to make him humane, and his sādhana if successful is highly reinforced, he is on his own. After the fashion of the child in the rhyme, when good he may be very very good (like St Francis) and when bad, homicidal (like Charles Manson or Gilles de Rais). Much of the institutional anxiety provoked by rationality- and convention-defying mystics comes from awareness of the disruptive potential which lies in deifying the intuitive and the ease with which dedicated mysticism degenerates into hubristic sorcery. In scoring atrocities, however, the righteous have probably beaten the sorcerers hollow through their own variety of hubris, a fact pointed out with relish by William Blake.

If nonethical "gnosis" is socially unsatisfying, positive demonism is a serious ideological hindrance to the cultivation of oceanic states—if more than one station is transmitting, our confidence that we are tuned to the right one is undermined, difficulties in the path of the yogi are put down to the sorcery of the Enemy, and the authority of ecclesiastical inspectorates is increased. Much of the religion-making drive and the emotional appeal of oceanic perception comes from its conviction of one-ness—any Manichean ideology would cast grave doubts on this, and much of the yogi's energy is diverted by it, if he persists, into struggling with a projected enemy.

Evil spirits in primitive religion are little more than the spiritual equivalent of local villains—organized spiritual crime, the cosmic Mafia, seems to have been first of all a Zoroastrian invention. Satan is strikingly quiet throughout the early books of the Old Testament—in these writings evil is either the result of human disobedience or, occasionally, part of the Divine purpose. Human gods, like human kings, rarely match up to the highest standards of human morality. It is God, not the Devil, who hardens Pharaoh's heart and gives bloodthirsty and revengeful orders; the Devil's debut in the *Book of Job* as a somewhat contumacious vizier or official is a probable legacy of the Babylonian captivity.

Just how much of the Christian tradition of demonism is Zoroastrian rather than Israelite in origin is vividly brought out by Zaehner,[43] himself an ancient Persian scholar and a Catholic, when he writes about the spiritual demonism of Bernanos. Indeed, heaven and hell too may have similar sources—they are not Israelite conceptions, and the Pharisees of the New Testament represent not so much the strict Jewish orthodoxy they claimed as the incorporation of Persian ideas: their name (*Perushim*—"separated") has probably nothing to do with Parsis or the like, but Victorian scholars devised etymologies to make the point.

The modern relevance of this is simply that it was the Devil who gave us objective science by rendering introspective experience suspect, separating the "objective world" and the unreliable flesh from the spiritual, and discouraging empirical and experimental mysticism, a point made forcibly by Blake. With a spiritual Mafia around, visionary experience has to be orthodox or risk believing diabolical disinformation. Hinduism had no such problems—the One, like the God of Moses, has terrific as well as benign aspects: part of the apparent philosophical indifference to evil and suffering consists of taking these in one's stride—they are unpleasant but part of the show. There are no autonomous devils, only bad human beings. The Asuras of Sanskrit literature, often rendered as "demons," are rather spoiled deities who practice all kinds of virtuous activity but fail to "know Brahman" because they are dualists at heart. Historically and etymologically they are in fact not *a-surans* (without-law) but Ahurans, the pre-Persian worshippers of Ahura-Mazda. From the other side, the Deva-worshipping, Sanskrit-speaking peoples who generated the Vedas appear in Zoroastrian scripture as nomadic bandits who were the scourge of rural Asia. More interesting, although Yama (Yima) the Hindu God of Death corresponds to the "first man" of the Gathas (who, being the first to die, became king of the next world) many other Vedic Gods are missing, probably because they had not yet appeared in folklore, and among these is Soma. The Vedic sages were boisterously shamanic, and Soma was the focus of their worship:

> Long-hair holds fire, holds the drug, holds
> heaven and earth.
> Long-hair opens everything under the sun. Long-hair
> declares it light.
>
> These sages, swathed in wind, put dirty red tatters on.
> When gods get in them, they ride with the rush of
> the wind.
>
> *Ṛg-Veda* 10.136

How far this psychedelic emphasis potentiated oceanic vision is anyone's guess, but by the time of the *Upaniṣads* introspection is primary, oceanic vision is the chief source of ontology, the godlets of Vedic times are engulfed in Brahman and good and evil are subordinated to vision. But further West psychedelic sages were associated with barbarian raiders and with Angra-Mainyu the Assaulting Spirit who inspired such misfortunes and operated through Evil-Mind (insanity). To a settled people suddenly subjected to the Aeshma, the catastrophic barbarian raid which the God of Right Thinking had been powerless to prevent, a supernatural dualism was a very natural conclusion—rather as it was to Bernanos seeing Christian Europe losing its mind in the First World War, or to Bonhoeffer in the Second. But from here a long fuse extends to St Paul wrestling with spiritual wickedness at the very top, to innumerable Christian saints whose introspective experience was blighted by concentration on resisting the assaults of the Devil, including their own sexuality, to the association of psychedelia of all kinds with witchcraft, and to the still-vigorous demonism of modern Catholic writers. Meister Eckhart, the witches of the sixteenth and seventeenth centuries, and even Dr Timothy Leary are all late casualties of an ancient tribal war, but so also, fortunately for Western empirical science, was the tradition of pharmacologically assisted introspection as a source of religious and philosophical knowledge. Pythagoras, Apollonius of Tyana, and possibly Plotinus might visit India and talk to oceanic sages, but the cultural lines were drawn. Cultural paranoia and mysticism are incompatible: moreover while oceanic states do not usually produce visions of Hell (apart from pharmacological bad trips in a culture already indoctrinated with it), depressive psychoses quite commonly do. Psychopathology is facilitated by any system of thought which sets guilt before shame and projects human defects on the absolute: sorcery, which attributes them to malicious humans, is probably the less harmful convention. In that sort of system, tapas really does become masochism, saints set out to punish rather than to manipulate the body and its mental consequences, aggression is turned inward, but at the same time the real world is set sufficiently apart from the mental for human empiricism to feel safe in investigating it. We do not often as scientists look at the ethnopsychology of our own "religion," and the "problem of evil" which bothered the ancient Zoroastrians when their world was disrupted by raiders is for us best addressed in terms of ethology and of social anthropology. If fear of the Devil had not demoralized the seekers of gnosis, and if the Greeks had not preferred arguing to meditating and getting high, we might never have got where we now are.

For Blake, poking around after "good" and "evil" pleases nobody but the devil, and constitutes the basic flaw. It is seeking for the knowledge of good and evil, not the mere fact of choosing evil, which damns man. It leads to the rule of Nobodaddy, the making of inane prohibitions, and the regime of Urizen's "iron books," by following the precepts of which we become corrupted into barbarous Druids who sacrifice people, Pharisaical oppressors of the poor, and suffer the entire repertoire of legalistic priestcraft. In fact, it is the religions which believe themselves to be the repositories of ethics, not the antinomian, who have the responsibility for most of the worst actions in human history. Rather than repeat the error laid on Adam and Eve by the "Great Selfhood," genuine ethics depend on genuine "intellect," which in Blake's diction presupposes both formal knowledge and, quintessentially, imagination: Los, not Urizen, is the genuine lawgiver, and the individual who had achieved a fusion of the four Blakeian "beings" would be effortlessly and undiscursively ethical because he would act with love, knowledge, feeling and imagination, in contrast to the standard manufacturers of ethics who propagate only their own inflated egos. This is a refreshingly original view when contrasted with the indifference of Hinduism and the guilt-orientation of formal Christianity, and is not far removed from the ethical humanism implicit in "good faith"— enlightened for Blake by his own brand of mystical experience.

Quite the most successful Christian-based incorporation of meditative, and potentially mystical, practice with ethical concern and practical commonsense is that of Quakerism, which we tend to overlook because it is close and lacks the appeal of exoticism. Ethical concern is the central "doctrine" of Quakerism and meditation its only "rite"—the use to be made of meditative experience is even more individual and empirical than in Hinduism, but Quaker acceptance of the possibility and value of a fusional outcome more closely approaches the Hindu than the Roman Catholic tradition. In an atheologic system there is no cause for disquiet if God is found to be within, nor do Quakers try to dictate how individual experience should be interpreted. Catholic mystics have much in common with sadhus and sannyasin (in the use of ritual, in a monasticism which accommodates career contemplatives, and in their interpretation of brahmācarya) and certain of their ecstatics were indistinguishable from yogis—St Joseph of Cupertino, for example. Quakers are by contrast "householders" in the Hindu sense of those whose meditative vocation is compatible with worldly responsibility and practical living—the Hindu "householder" is by tradition a ritualist, however: Quakers reject ritual, monasticism, ecclesiastical institutions and dogmatic formulations altogether. They also reject the distaste of the meditative Hindu "householder" for worldly concerns (he, as a rule, while doing what is expected of him, comes as near to living a monastic life as his responsibilities permit). The Quaker view is closer to *sahāja*, it treats human activities as inherently sacramental, so that it needs no sacraments to single some of them out in this particular, and it is one of the few religious modes which bases its postures on concerned common sense. Like the Tantriks, Quakers have occasionally felt it necessary to flout social and religious convention: their unaggressive firmness in standing on principle over matters such as nonviolence has made the most arbitrary governments think twice before taking them on. They have not eroticized mysticism, but would have no difficulty in seeing sexuality, in a responsible setting, as a source of mystical experience. Their practical success has been accompanied by a far greater degree of social concern than the "way-of-earthly-prosperity" in Hindu tradition. There is a popular belief among some Hindus in yogic or meditative practice as a form of magic to produce prosperity, which treats business success as siddhī rather than as a normal result of hard work and square dealing. Some American business evangelicals treat

I and That

prayer in the same way. If the Quaker tradition incorporated Blake's sometimes perfervid imagination in place of deliberate understatement, or had kept the psychedelic tone of its very early days, it might appeal more to the revived contemplative impulse in our society than it has done so far: Blake and the Quakers are saying many of the same things, but Quakerism rejects poetic hyperbole as insincere, and their attitude is basically too serious for counterculture-type expression, even though it did at one time represent a very definite counterculture protest itself. It is easier for the counterculture to swallow a meditative practice based in an exotic religious tradition, which it doesn't understand, rather than in any Christian tradition, "Christianity" being a system which has been presented to it dogmatically, and which it consequently rejects. To the extent that Quaker tradition represents both concerned responsibility ("love") and autonomy (though its origination is Christian, any given person's Christology is a matter for personal experience) it really escapes most strictures on Christianity in general. Quakers would never have jailed, or ostracized, Meister Eckhart because for God's sake he took leave of God.

"Going in for ethics is for man an integral part of the role of the taught or the authority-acceptor, without the existence of which his cultural sociogenetic evolutionary system could not operate":[51] in other words, we are ethically programmed because we are social animals, but the content of our ethic is not—what is programmed is a space to hold cultural programming, adapted to our status as an organism which operates more, in the evolutionary sense, on Lamarkian, culture-derived behaviors than on built-in instinctual repertoires: where these exist they are subject always to a social override so large that not even our gender identity depends on chromosomal sex. The sensitivity of the social animal to "rightness," however, is there in a magnified form, and it interacts with the complexity of early psychosexual development to make us obsessionally prone to guilt, and the enactment of morally-colored rituals which are both ethically and adaptively irrelevant—the rules of Urizen.

In fact, of all Urizen's rules, the only interesting one biologically is the prohibition of incest. This looks as if it should be instinctually adaptive; but, as Freud realized, we do not need rules where we have well-defined instincts; and man has *no* "instinctual" block to consanguineous mating, which is not uncommon despite the cultural unanimity against it. This rule is better seen as a projection of a special-situation anxiety arising from human childhood—the rule has probably had adaptive consequences, and these might indirectly have served to perpetuate what appears to be the biology that gives rise to it. Beyond this, all identity-exploring religions ultimately replace ethics where they belong, in the individual human *qua* social animal, who has need of ethicity as a manifestation of his identity within a social species, over against fellow humans. Ethical sense ("righteousness"), and some experience of identity are not human "markers"—all social animals exhibit one, and perhaps both. Dogs are aware of the "opinion" and the social feedback of other dogs. Humans project dominance out into the nonhuman because it controls and can surprise or threaten them by its initiatives, as a dog can be surprised by its master and even killed by him. It is because our facility of projection has personalized randomness and taken it, as it were, into the family or pack wherein ethical reactions are biologically rooted[52,53,54] that we project the source and sanction of righteousness outside ourselves and our immediate context and contacts—we are dogs who have invented themselves a master. Had dogs done so, they might, if naive about humans, have made him in their own image. Dogs who have had a master introject his human requirements. Our "master" was captious, capricious and unpredictable as nonhuman processes are, when viewed by human consequences; but in humanizing the nonhuman we had to give it a magnified version of human ethical requirement, as we shared with rocks and animals the αἰδὼς proper to people. In viewing the sophisticated and convoluted religious philosophies and behaviors of today, it could well be upon simple processes such as these that we should concentrate in defining what exactly we mean by "man's encounter with the sacral."

The promise of survival, by contrast, whether regarded as a privilege or a doubtful blessing, seems to inhere in the relationship of religion to the I-experience. The compelling illusion of autonomy from the body seems to subsume the illusion of permanence apart from the body, whether in a hell, a Valhalla, or as a ghost. The role of the experience of death, which perplexes even elephants and chimpanzees when it is seen in a comrade, is clearly formative of a whole range of behaviors. I include it here only insofar as its religious influence seems strongly connected with the identity experience. Both it and the ceremonies with which it has been surrounded are functionally *rites de passage* (even Californians talk of "passing" or "passing over," terms reserved for our only other valid *rite de passage*, the academic examination). In these rites we see "religion" defending the one-ness of the I, while in mysticism the I so reinforced examines and explores its potential multiplicity—including in its experience oceanic sensations which make vulgar immortalisms no longer relevant because "all is always now," the reaction seen by Grof in his terminal patients treated with LSD.[55]

IX
Religion and death

The unique human experience of I-ness is combined with the realization that I-ness is limited in time. The child's confrontation with death postdates the acquisition of I-ness by only a few years. Death may well be the most important formative factor in human behaviors, because it is foreseen. With the prevision comes a range of responses, all of them falling within the range of behaviors which we have termed religious—appeasement of the not-I so that the lease of our surviving individualities may be prolonged, dialogue with the dead, who once possessed individuality and who may or may not continue to possess it, together with magical power: denial of the transience of I-ness itself expressed in various personal eschatologies: and finally in the oceanic experience, which appears to possess a particular efficacy in restructuring the human fear of death.

Personal eschatologies are as old as man. They begin with the simple convention of the departure on a journey, calling for gravegoods and the company of beloved animals or persons—soon replaced, since this is a magical, or "as if" journey, by less expensive substitutes—effigies, *ushabti* the "answerers" of Egyptian burials, spirit goods. As the journey itself becomes the matter for human imagination, it merges with the shamanic journey, differing from the harrowing of hell only in that the traveler does not return, as does the shaman—here the shaman acts for the generality as the old-time scout acted for the pioneer train: he finds the trail and comes back. It is from this visionary source that Egyptian religion drew its detailed instructions to the dead on how they should comport themselves on reaching the other world. To this body of conviction and detailed instruction the experiences of the dream, and the "astral" sensations not uncommon in serious illness short of death, may well have contributed detail.

Humans normally deny death if they can: in other words, they elect to believe that the compelling experience of I-ness cannot be transient, and they experience the possibility of its being so in terms of terrifying isolation, annihilation or castration. Austere religions such as Judaism have rejected the more naive denials—the righteous are in the hands of God, they do not need to fear torment, but neither should they expect their I-ness to outlive their body; at best they depend on the uncovenanted ability of God to raise up whom He will, and on the prospect of surviving in offspring and tribal memory, as part of a moral Van Allen Belt surrounding future generations.

Sophisticated cultures ultimately attenuate even the attenuated beliefs of their folk predecessors about partial, lemurial survival, of the kind which made Achilles in Hades say that he would rather be a poor man's serf than a king among ghosts. Much the same has happened in our culture to the robuster heaven and hell of medieval iconography—few now seriously believe in the literalism which links continued I-ness with the resurrection of the body: contemporary Christians have long tended to replace the orthodox idea of resurrection with that of inherent immortality, originally pagan.

At the point, however, where mythologies of denial begin to run out of steam, cultures not uncommonly begin to bring death itself into focus as a religious experience. These attempts are both psychologically and intellectually far more interesting than are the denial mythologies, whether these are of the simple kind (the dead are not really dead) or of the elaborate, in terms of Platonic speculation, transmigrationist ideas of recycling, or the like. The basic fact is that I-ness is our chief possession, about to be extinguished at some time. About this we may theorize, or we may, and usually do, choose to ignore it. However, when it comes to the crunch, the individual faced with the likelihood of dying now recapitulates the progress of religious ideas in society. Starting from naive denial, he moves to appeasement ("not me, not this time"), to indignant despair, to mourning, and finally—and this seems to be the optimal resolution—to an experiential acceptance. Long before "thanatology" was developed for death-shy middle-class people in prosperous countries whose main hazard was no longer infection or violence but cancer, Tolstoy depicted this sequence in *The Death of Ivan Ilyitch*. In a more doctrinally determined setting, Cardinal Newman, assisted by Elgar, makes it vividly actual in *The Dream of Gerontius*. What is usually forgotten about *Gerontius* is that it is a dream, not an account of the journey of the soul. The religious manifestations of eschatology—judgment, reconciliation, self-discovery, "knowing as we are known"—which religion traditionally locates *post mortem* are in fact *ante mortem* experiences, occurring while we are still there to experience, and far more important than the astral illusions experienced by some of Kübler-Ross's *revenants*. The fact is that awareness of an impending end to I-ness performs an operation on the boundaries of I-ness as major as any mystical experience though less dramatic, if only by cutting down our personal investments in triviality. Death must accordingly, by our definition, be rated as a religious experience—not because we are religiose about it, but because both death itself and the involved contemplation of it perform operations upon self as against not-self.

The sharpening of experience by impending death, which is for many people their first experience of existential "good faith," and which makes the conduct of group psychotherapy with terminal patients such a profound and moving experience[56] is at the level of conscious introspection. Mysticism, where it attains the suspension of I-ness, introduces a different modality, but one with similar effects. It is universally agreed by oceanic mystics that the experience of nondifference abolishes the fear of death, insofar as that is a fear of the loss of identity. In fact, many people who have a penchant towards fusional experience stop or avoid it because the threat of suspended I-ness is too like what they fear of death. Once experienced, however, it can clearly restructure attitudes in many ways: in the oceanic experience I-ness is suspended with none of the catastrophically distressing feelings of separation, castration and so on which we attribute to not-being. If one becomes empathically aware, first, that I-ness is a hallucinatory not an ontological "structure," and second that its suspension does not suspend experience, it is a small step to the assumption that death itself is a reacquisition of the oceanic bliss in perpetuity—*maha samādhi*. This is a naive reassurance in view of the fact that in samādhi perception itself does not stop—it is only altered in quality. A less naive consequence of samādhi, however, is that the concept of linear time is intuitively perceived as being also a hallucination: a large part of our distaste for death centers on a quantitative element—we want more time, more of the same; a profound sensation that "all is always now" basically reorders this anxiety. If the idea that "death is only samādhi" is a mystical cop-out, this reordering is not. It is a reordering sought by other means during the last part of terminal illness—in the foreshortening of time, the attempt to live ten years in two years of real time—and by all of us throughout life in the cultivation of experiences which are in fact mini-lives, alternative lives foreshortened, the equivalents of *amours de voyage*, in which the speed of communication, of experience and of intimacy may equal those of dream experience—a kind of high-speed morse. The oceanic reordering of our valuation of time, permanence and duration is more radical, however, and depends on the structure which we have attributed to I-ness as a time-based phenomenon—the mystic does not verbalize the nature of this structural relationship, but he does intuit it schematically, since one thing which the unmodified analog path can probably do is to intuit its own structure in nonverbal terms. This once "seen" as an empathic dissolution of time-as-linear and time-as-quantity is a profoundly reordering experience.

The epic journey of Gilgamesh was undertaken to find a remedy for death—which, when found, was eaten by a snake; the journey provided not magic but reconciliation. This version of the shamanic voyage is more sophisticated than the Homeric or Dantesque forms. The shaman encounters the "remedy for death" by facing dissolution of identity and finding that it is pleasant, not unpleasant, that I-ness can be seen as a subjective illusion not a cherished possession, and that whether time is limited for us or endless depends on how we feel about time. This is the mystical core—superadded is the dream experience—journey, ordeals, encounters with projected selves—which subsumes both life-as-journey and the accelerated journey undertaken just premortally by paśu like Ivan Ilyitch, who do not start moving spiritually until it is almost closing time (one would like to infer that in a culture more ritually conscious, the journey-of-life and the journey of Gerontius and his psychopomp would coincide, and not need the terminal sprint to get under the gate).

One needs to be careful in starting the ball rolling about death as a religious experience. One can easily imagine the same pollyannic literature as that which suggests that parturition is a super-orgasm if undertaken in the right frame of mind. Thanatology of this sort is after a general anesthetic for deathbed use, when it ought to be taking the more austere view that there is nothing like lifelong confrontation with mortality to preserve our genuineness of intention and our impatience with the trivial. Few people in our culture get to realize that all experience is sacral until they are pronounced about to die. For all the pathetic circumlocutions by which "religions" have tried to show that death does not happen or does not matter, its religious significance, judged by its efficacy in shaping and reshaping the bound between I and That, is highest where we admit that it does happen, will happen, and will happen to us, so that in Russell's terms we live on the solid foundation of an unshakeable despair—despair of preserving our I, that is, in a mummified form by any kind of sorcery. The consequence of real death is that all experience is sacral because it is limited and irreversible—only an immortal or an inordinately long-lived organism could afford a secular category of experience which did not really require seriousness.

Philosophy normally does very little for the human unease over death, beyond providing a posture of mortalist stoicism. The introspection of mystics, however, whether primitive or sophisticated, introduces something quite new, namely the empirical observation that time, and consequently the entire linearity of commonsense experience, are conditional. Much of the history of human religions appears to reflect an interchange between straightforward denial mythologies, incorporated into many popular religions, and the impressive experience of individuals who then try to communicate to those who have not shared that experience that they are asking the wrong question. Popular Christianity has adopted the idea of "eternal life" as a linear continuation of temporal experience "in Heaven," either after a future resurrection or as an inherent property of "the soul." This belief was not part of the Jewish tradition, and it is interesting to notice the answers of Jesus to questions about it—"I myself am the resurrection and the life" . . . "my father's house has many rooms in it" . . . and "about the resurrection of the dead, whether they really do rise from the grave, remember God is not the god of the dead but of the living. You have got it entirely wrong." These sound less like the endorsement of linear immortalism than the attempts of a seer to convey that naive views of endless or limited life are made irrelevant by the content of the oceanic experience—"ye do greatly err" is addressed not only to the Sadducees but to both sides in the dispute—if the intuitive view of time is simply a result of a human mode of perception, they are asking a meaningless question, similar to the anxieties of those who expected circumnavigators to fall off the edges of a flat earth. "Eternal life" has meaning, but it is not so much joined on to linear–individualist experience as at right angles to it.

How far this kind of consolation is apt to the death-anxieties of modern societies one cannot predict. Nor can one say whether it could replace the mythologies of denial: these have long been in retreat before the growing knowledge of the neural bases of experience and the consequent implausibility of disembodied intelligences. As a theoretical realization drawn from physics, or from books like this, a revised view of the meaning of time and of duration lacks flesh—the energetic theory of matter does not make the world seem less real, and it is basically the habitual mode of experience, which is, after all, the style of humanness, which most people fear to lose; boddhisattvas like Jesus, if indeed this is the import of his teachings, abstained from demolishing more simplistic consolations probably on the ground that they were right in effect (we need not fear transience) if not in literal substance. I have yet to see a terminally ill patient reconciled by, say, T. S. Eliot's awareness that:

> "the end precedes the beginning
> and all is always now."

The direct experience of oceanic vision is another matter, precisely because it is an experience, while a mythology or a philosophy are not. It is quite possibly the fact that such a dissolution of conventional experience, not only of seriality but of I-ness, answers the human anxiety over death which has made it so important in religion-making. Gautama left home because of it. Being moreover empirical, experienced and hard-nosed in that it leads to a direct comprehension of how human perceptions structure the apparently objective world, it actually appeals to the objectivism which it supplants, and early experiments with psychedelic agents in terminal illness suggested that the change of view, because it is nondiscursive, works equally well in people who are not particularly interested in the epistemology of "the objective." It may be for our time. To this the mystic contributes only the empathic awareness that I-ness can be otherwise looked at, and that when it is so looked at, death does not "matter" in quite the way it did, gods, heavens and theologies are a clumsy shorthand, and that I-ness as present in the human brain is all-encompassing without arrogance or self-deification. One precipitant of this experience, or reordering of experience, is the prospect of death itself—by setting off a motivated and engaged introspection of what I-ness is. Very clearly the sages who sought samādhi in burning-grounds were not morbid, any more than those who practiced tapāsya were merely masochistic. The ikon in which this truth is embodied is not that of Christ upon the Cross, in which sacrifice atones. It is rather, or also, that of the Goddess Kālī, Devouring Time personified—shocking to Western susceptibility, but invested with great psychological power. A beautiful woman, four-armed, black, with an expression combining laughter, ferocity and sexual excitement, she is the dissolver of everything including the illusion of self.

> "Most fearful, her laughter shows her dreadful teeth. She stands upon a corpse. She has four arms. Her hands hold a sword and a head, and show the gestures of *removing fear* and *conferring boons*. She is the auspicious goddess of sleep, the wife of Siva.
> "Naked, clothed only in space, the goddess shines. Her tongue protrudes. She wears heads for a necklace. In this form one should meditate on the power of Time, Kālī, who lives near the funeral pyres."[57]

It would be difficult to give the whole discursive input of this ikon. Sufficient to say that whoever can address that which dissolves I-ness, whether it be sword, fire, meditation, sexuality or devouring time and do so without fear, can experience the conferring of boons and the loss of anxiety in the mortal condition.

X

Postscript: Medicine and I-ness

The concern of psychiatry with identity is evident—it is part of the stock in trade of the "existential" and "humanistic" modes: it is for this reason surprising that so little interest has focused on its mechanism, and so much on its social and behavioral expressions. Medicine, on the other hand, has a traditional and intuitive awareness of the bodily consequences of factors which affect, or operate through, the sensation of identity, starting with the universal clinical observation that not only does "mind" markedly affect body, but changes in body image quite commonly produce effects on body function. The standard instruction given to students that one must "treat the whole person," that placebo effects make up much of therapy, and that numerous physical states can be induced by "suggestion," are really other ways of putting the same thing. Their *lumpen*-character has been due not to laziness so much as to lack of documentation of what has really been going on: many physicians have had a clinical impression that malignancy could be furthered, if not actually induced, by a state of mind, and possibly even on occasion cured by one, but beyond a general awareness that states of mind influence hormonal patterns and metabolism, as well as being influenced by them, it was difficult to see how other than anecdotal impressions could be documented. Observation of the reality of central control over "involuntary" or autonomic processes by biofeedback or operant conditioning comes opportunely to link hands with psychotheoretical speculations—originally Reichian—about interaction between body image and disease states, in that these are made investigable and theoretically plausible rather than speculative at the psychoanalytic level. Good doctors have for years tried to do something about modifying the body image of over-tense or accident-prone people in order to control their physical dysfunctions, but have not usually put it quite like that.

The extreme dissolution of I-ness pursued by mystics also dissolves the body image as separate from what is not body, and Hindu yoga, aside from some grandiose claims to control health and longevity, has had little concern with physical well-being: sadhus tend to claim that in the preliminary exercises which they undertake to gain control over voluntary ecstasy they also acquire almost total voluntary control over their health, but these alleged powers rate as *siddhi*, or magic tricks, on a par with magical feats such as levitation, and not worthy of the serious attention of the ecstasy-directed adept save as a means to further samādhi. The true situation seems to be that many ecstatics using traditional yogas acquire ability to monitor autonomic processes without using an external display, and thus make some of them accessible to biofeedback. What they can actually accomplish in this way, and how far the same devices could be used for therapy rather than in manipulating the sense of identity, remains unclear.

Medicine is the practical activity which most concerns itself with body, body image, and the practically important alterations of physical self-experience, and its form invariably reflects the "religion," or schematic I–That perception, current in the culture where it exists, in both doctor and patient. It is accordingly quite the most interesting test case for the implications of the objectivist "religion" and the style which goes with it. Where that style has imposed social distortions, objectivism itself, moreover, tends to have recourse to medicine—in this case psychiatry. One feature of objectivism–technologism is that while it is highly successful in pursuing short-term objectives, it is basically aimless for want of an integrative emphasis. Technology is played as a game for its own sake, but the overall priorities which the techniques are applied to realize are naive, trivial or, in the case of politics, commercialism and military technology, frankly demonic and anti-human. In the diction of scientism itself they are "psychopathic" or "deranged"—terms borrowed from medicine and the normative concept of *health*. While earlier styles would have attributed Nazism, Stalinism, the atomic bomb and the Viet Nam war successively to demonic possession, wickedness and unreason, we attribute them to psychopathology.

It has been medicine, moreover, which—by the infusion of depth psychology, and later of "existential" philosophy—finds itself among the first practical disciplines to run into trouble with the objective model and the machine analogy. Psychiatry now has to live with contradiction in recognizing contexts where the machine analogy holds, and dysfunctions respond to behavior therapy or chemical agents, and those, familiar to every pretechnical physician and to good modern physicians however competent in science, where it does not—with the proviso that in almost all illness, physical and non-physical or body-image-dependent factors demonstrably coexist.

Many of the non-theistic religious systems, such as group encounter, "humanistic psychology" and other charismatic rituals that would formerly have taken their sanction from religion now take it from psychiatry or "health." It may be that because medicine is the discipline in which I was trained that I see it as critically situated in the emergence of a new style of self-perception, but the possibility has independent weight. For that reason I have concluded this discussion of the nature and biology of religious behaviors by considering medicine in particular.

One context in which the relationship of I with That is of practical importance is the context of self-cure. The return of Western thought, under the escort of science, to re-examine archaic forms of inner manipulation has owed little to the search for spiritual wholeness, but it has owed a great deal to neuro-psychiatry and to the investigation of self-manipulative substitutes for external medication—biofeedback in particular. Not only have the doctor and the neurologist given cultural permission to the yogi—medicine in its wider sense, by introducing hallucinogens and investigating their actions, restored an unexpected and quite uncontrollable revival of interest in oceanic states and the nature of the identity experience in ontology. It now may well face a change in its own style from either/or (magic or science) to both/and, depending on the practical efficacy of non-pharmacological maneuvers which it has so far discounted *ex hypothesi*.

There is no theoretical reason why sufficiently active manipulation of the body image should not in fact alter physically programmed characteristics such as longevity. Metabolic rate is quite possibly manipulatable in this way, and the sensor which "reads" caloric intake and modifies the rate of aging in rodents[58] is quite possibly hypothalamic. There is no theoretical reason why malignancy should not be similarly influenced—not only in site, as it can be by social factors in mice acting on the hormonal cycle, but also by immune processes, since these appear to be equally under central control and modifiable by conditioning.[59,60] The $64,000 question is whether, and how reliably, they can in fact be so modified.

The discussion of the therapeutic manipulation of mind may seem misplaced in a discussion of religion, but in fact it belongs there phylogenetically if not in current parlance. Yogic mystics are unusual in not being very interested in their own or other people's health—the shaman, however, is the ancestor of the physician, operating at the interface of I and body, as well as at the other boundaries of the I. He uses a traditional repertoire of I-modifying methods aimed at the body image, which look a lot more theoretically interesting, in spite of the mystification and hocus which often attends them, the more we recognize what precisely he is doing. Not having pharmacological ways of affecting body function directly, or having few of them, and knowing nothing about pathophysiology, the traditional "healer" is obliged to operate through the body image and its perception by the I, as the only site which he has the technology to tackle.

In the last century medicine has figured as the star turn of socially valuable applications arising from objective science—one which has escaped corruption. A number of writers have pointed out—not always with the antimedical bias of Bernard Shaw or Ivan Ilyitch—that the popular view of curative medicine as the fount from which our improved health has sprung over the last century is probably an illusion: limitation of family size, increase in food supply, and a better physical environment were probably more important, in that order.[61] Certainly the disorders now most in evidence are life-style generated and are not particularly susceptible to curative medicine.[62]

In fact, this is not evidence of the failure of therapeutics, but rather of their success *in the context in which they evolved*. Modern medicine and its technology were developed as an answer to the surgical and infective conditions which plagued the nineteenth century, resulting in the deaths of numerous young adults and making it common that of eight or ten children only four or five would be reared. Every Victorian household had a fairly intimate acquaintance with premature death. When the popular Prince Consort of England died of typhoid, after organizing Britain's greatest exhibition of technology, *The Times* described medicine as "the withered arm of science." Anti-infective medicine, pioneered by Koch, Ehrlich, Pasteur and Lister, was the answer to this social demand—surgery was its spinoff, for the restraint on surgical technique was infection. The application of chemistry and technology to the human body paid off. One of their consequences was the obscuring of the eighteenth-century idea of "right living" as a means of self-care, and the patient's own responsibility for the avoidance of disease. Health maxims could not prove their value in the epidemic presence of typhoid and inoperable appendicitis. The success of technological medicine had the same consequence in forming the patient's attitude to his body as technology in general had in forming public attitudes to the environment—both were machine-like and could be fixed by experts. Because our attempts to fix them succeeded in the limited missions which they undertook (medicine dealt with infections, industry provided consumer affluence) we are now left with the un-fixables, as a form of discovered check. Students who shy off neurology because there is no specific therapy for the commonest neurological disorders, such as multiple sclerosis, do not realize that this is so because the chief neurological disorder of the last century, neurosyphilis, is now treatable and preventable.

It is evident, however, that the criticism is valid, in that though a few further fixes may be forthcoming (immunology may deal with multiple sclerosis, for example) we need a new set of medical goals and a new attitude to health maintenance, apt to an order in which typhoid is rare, major surgery easy—sometimes too easy—and motor accidents, suicide, cardiovascular disease, and environmentally generated neoplasms kill those whom typhoid and surgical conditions would formerly have claimed. An updated version of the healthy-living rules of the eighteenth century might now show results, but this would require a revision of our attitude toward our bodies and our responsibility for their maintenance difficult to achieve. It is simpler to look for one-shot chemotherapies, however unlikely, against irrational diet, lack of exercise and cigarette-generated neoplasia while staying with our present life style.

A medical orientation which sets about modifying the patient's perception of self and body image, and which combines these goals with quasi-ethical prohibitions and counsels regarding attitude toward living, has many of the characters which we have here attributed to religion. Blake's concept of enlightenment coming by way of the tempering or union of the Four Zoas is apposite to the task of much psychotherapy, though we might be prepared to add a fifth, namely social responsibility or the need for interaction and valuation by others, which does not fall within the sphere of Blake's four-way division. Our medicine, being specifically and historically task-oriented, and at the same time operating in a scientific-industrial culture, is certainly the medicine of Urizen, or insightless scientism, so long as it regards health as solely a technological rather than a social and personal problem. Most contemporary nonmedical spiritual healers of the Californian type replace Urizen with Tharmas ("sensate focus," nondenial of bodily pleasure)—Christian healers combine Urizen (dogma and moralism) with genuflection to *bhakti* (Luvah, the personification of passions, devotional or secular). The integrative "spirit" of Blake's pantheon, Los, the faculty of imaginative intellect, is not a popular personage in any of the therapeutic schools, conventional or unorthodox, but he seems due for incorporation into them. In Blake's eschatology, Locke and Newton, who personify scientism, combine with Milton and Chaucer, representing imagination, to complete a repertoire of attitudes which are complementary to each other in constituting "intellect" and only dangerous or negative when they reflect distortion through overconcentration on one human faculty.

Rather than allow the antimedical to discourage us by pointing to the low social effectiveness of technical medicine in prevention, we should be inquiring into the relatively good results which our prescientific forbears obtained out of great therapeutic poverty, because anything they could do, we could do much better: not only because of the fact that we have genuine therapeutics where they did not, but because we have the apparatus to do discursively what they did intuitively, and make it a great deal less hit-and-miss. It is always sad when discussion of the clinical future, and of what we mean by clinical judgment, recedes from this particular insight—Feinstein's well-meaning exposition of clinical judgment as statistically-based scientific therapeutics and only that is a case in point.[63] We now know that every patient has not only a body but a body image—so that there is a computer inside setting up health or disease, ranging from insanity to cancer to broken legs to querulous immaterial complaints. We can deal with some of the consequences of its activities when these become overt, but we ignore the fact that it is also programmable—often by apparent irrelevancies which spring from our therapeutic attitude, and reflect cultural biases nosogenic in their implications which our therapeutics share with the patient. We know that clinical behaviors which are rigidly "scientific" can also be irrepressibly anthropological—we wear masks for one cultural reason, wizards for another, but masks are masks: doctor and nurse, the nineteenth-century dyad, operated in a culture where father/mother or father/hired nannie had experiential meaning for the patient and could invoke benign regression or bad vibrations.

California contains today the world's most experienced patients. Everyone we see will accordingly have had some encounters with medicine, and many will have supplemented it with "healing." It is instructive, if one is not familiar with them, to take time to ascertain from them the precepts and methods of their particular healer—not simply to show willing, or to head off risky dietary and other fads, but to examine what the popular "healer" is actually doing. In general he or she will be found to offer the same repertoire as do healers in naive cultures, plus a stronger element of theory apt to patients who have been brought up on the scientific–discursive view—forces, energies and the like rather than ghosts or spirits. The basic armamentarium of such a healer is fourfold. There are rules, prohibitions, singularities and "supportive ingestibles" ranging from herbs to organic vegetables—some of these are just possibly therapeutic in a physical sense, the sense in which medical bottles of tonic and injunctions to take exercise are physically therapeutic, but their main functions are to give support and to concentrate the mind. There is an as-if system, usually now in a discursive or pseudo-scientific guise, which offers an integrative explanation, preferably a novel one. Its function is not to "explain" disease in the sense that bacteriology has "explained" tuberculosis or nutritional studies explain rickets. What it normally does is to effect an attitudinal reorientation toward the patient's own body and body image: going along with the "as-if" model has sensate-focus effects plus the coherence given by an explanation (any explanation) and in our culture explanation is a sacrament.

"Fringe" medical systems run to ideologies, where they are not wholly arbitrary, and these ideologies differ on examination from science in the omission of the words "as if"—they confuse analogy with objective fact. "Sexual attractions between man and woman represent bipolar bioelectric energy," "energy flows from healer to healed," "Lying naked on bare soil you draw energy from the ground or place yourself in touch with nature," are not factual but analogic statements, and the "energy" in question is a metaphor—in the laying-on of hands what passes is less like energy than like information, if we want to be technical about it. The ascent of the spinal chakras by the kundalini-force in conventional yoga is another as-if process, more interesting in that unlike their Californian followers Hindu thinkers did not confuse the objective body with the "subtle body"—they were talking about a body image manipulation. Anyone who has tried to communicate what exactly is the mental maneuver which alters blood-flow in biofeedback experiments will recognize the convenience of a "sensate focus" shorthand, however much this may confuse the naive between physiology and mental imaging.

Cultures have their own ways of reifying analogy to express experience, and symptoms can be one such way. What we often forget is that at a discursive level scientific objectivism is *our* culture's way of doing so. It has paid off abundantly, but in dealing with anything as subtle as the interaction of physiology, pathology and self-perception, where manipulations of the body image have sizeable and so far uncharted effects on function, it has limitations. Doctors have tackled this so far at the intuitive level, but they need instruction in cultural anthropology, otherwise useful psychotherapeutic resources are left to mystifying quacks.

Next in the repertoire are exercises of mind or body reinforcing the "as-if" experience, and often giving permission and validation to the patient's feelings of being alienated from, neglected by, or misunderstood by, straight social resources, medicine included. These serve to effect a break with previous, often mechanistic, body-perceptions. Lastly there is charisma—high-intensity nonverbal communication, the laying-on of hands, the radiation of personhood by a larger than lifesize person.

What contemporary shamans have done is to reorder intuitively to the beliefs and body-attitudes of our culture (attitudes many of them the unwitting work of medicine) a traditional repertoire which is reasonably effective in the supportive management of symptoms which are self-limiting, or sociogenic, or aggravated by attitude. It is also effective, if it is not too eccentric in the "as-if" positions which it takes, in helping patients to escape from body image problems reified, or actually expressed, as symptoms. Nor can one entirely exclude preventive value in major diseases—only a very hardy pathologist would now ignore the possibility that even tumor induction can on occasion reflect body image problems—cardiovascular disease almost certainly does, under the general rubric of "stress."

This does not suggest that physicians go to sit at the feet either of the late Edgar Cayce or of the late Kathleen Kuhlman, but it might suggest that the structure of traditional healing is relevant to scientific therapeutics, even though the validity of its "as-if" statement is not. The tendency so far has been either to believe these as facts or to dismiss them as nonsense—the real point would be to examine what exactly they bring about.

The relation of I and That is important in all simple cultures, and the physician (usually, at this point, a shaman) is the interface man. His expertise is in helping us handle the not-I: diseases result from breaking taboos, which are practical, not moral matters—if you eat kangaroo you offend the kangaroo spirit, rather as if you handle plutonium you offend the plutonium spirit, and in either case you are made sick—or they result from the sorcery of other humans. Both spirits and malicious humans are part of the not-self. The origin of sorcery in our society lies more in an objectified social order than in malignant individuals. In highly structured cultures, religion is doctrinal and block-like, and many complaints which we reify as malaise or illness and take to the physician are transferred to the religious level as sins for purposes of exorcism or confession.

In putting most of these anthropological resources behind us we have gained a great deal in control of specific ill health. Where we do less well is with the not very sick, or not yet very sick, in psychophysical set. They make up the bulk of our practice, and inappropriate recourse to scientism can give them real sicknesses, such as drug dependence or iatrogenic disability. Non-dogmatic, changing societies throw the individual on his own limited resources and those of immediate contacts—with "society" his contacts are social but nontouching: being touched by a stranger is an unusual and sacramental experience. Those who are "religious" in such conditions are non-dogmatic and empirical—their religion is arrived at by inner experience—and it happens that religious empirics are traditionally into the exploration of inner structure through body image manipulation, whether they be shamans or practitioners of Tantrik yoga. Shamans are quite often healers (usually of others, occasionally of themselves): yogis in general are not; though they carry out considerable physiological manipulations, these are directed to a special end, the sensation of nondifference from reality. Be that as it may, the choice of empiricism-based, try-it-and-see, religions is apt to the times—for a start, it is not very different from the empirical approach of science. There too, we try it and see.

We may well wonder what this has to do with office medicine. The point is that the area of function of such self-manipulations is the area covering the effects of anxiety, dissatisfaction, so-called growth experiences, which can be painful as well as rewarding, adaptation to change, resentment of society and sorcery conducted by others, an area which we in our culture have been taught to manipulate by drugs. It is not a field where drugs are of primary effect, though these may control the diseases which are end-products—indeed, the fact of being touched by the doctor, looked at by him, and receiving communication from him can affect them more, and we at present often let the content of that communication take care of itself. Some of us in England have had illuminating experiences of dealing with educated Nigerians who were suffering from the effects of sorcery. The effects were physical, but it was no use giving them pills. We see few bewitched Americans, even after *The Exorcist*—or do we? Old people are the victims of black magic, which decrees that they ought to be crazy, useless or impotent, and may if they are susceptible make them so. Black people have been victims of a form of sorcery known as race prejudice—and may possibly owe a high incidence of hypertension to it, in part at least.

Taking responsibility for our bodily health is a weighty business, weightier than the eighteenth century realized, for it assumed that the Reasonable Man's desire for health was unalloyed, whereas we recognize that self-destructive behaviors are real, and that diseases can provide revenge, excuse, and communication which may be actively if unconsciously sought. Just as the pregnant teenager who does not use easily available contraception may be displaying motives more complex than mere negligence, most of the causes of sociogenic disease can be actively pursued in a way that smallpox, plague and peritonitis were not—the diseases we have removed were lottery items, while those which now require attention have more of the character of Russian roulette.

It is here that the healer scores. He does reorder the body image, he imposes religiose maxims of practice and abstinence, he attacks conventional lifestyles, all old shamanic resources: his shamanism is in itself a therapeutic advantage, for the shaman is an expert in demonic manifestations and demons are self-destructive behaviors reified. By contrast we risk papering over symptoms and giving the demons their head—we order tranquillizers instead of reordering lifestyles and sleeping pills instead of cutting down environmental noise and social competition. Our response to cigarette addiction is not confrontation but the search for cancer cures and the tar-free cigarette.

It is both evident and salutary that in medicine as in general, a new perception of ontology and a new assessment of the nature of I and of That should come to succeed the religion of objectivism. That religion was a necessary stage in the deepening comprehension of human functioning and human requirements: our awareness of limitations upon mechanism as a self-view and a world view is now a scientific, not an intuitive or nondiscursive awareness. It results from a devoted application of the principle of abstraction and verification to the point at which, like the "cosmic serpent," it begins to feed upon its own tail and initiate a change in self-awareness and cultural style. We may respect "naturals" like Blake who perceived the wider pattern by native vision, but we have been obliged to come to the same position the hard way—there is a certain self-denying good faith and rejection of the pleasant and the facile in the formulation of truth which is the one inherent moral value of science; that nonsense, however grandiloquent, is nonsense still, and that when a "religion," or the style of a period, is perceived to be nonsense, then either we have misunderstood the universe of discourse, or we are dealing with bad faith. In medicine there is no going back to magic or to empirical quackery. If meditation cures cancer, we want to see statistics, and our statistical methods are now sophisticated enough not to be short-circuited by attributing failures to unbelief or the wrong attitude of mind. If in fact it proves true that there are large resources of body-manipulation which could be tapped by a better comprehension of the structure of identity, there is no single finding which could do more to focus our attention on inner space: if not, identity and its structure retain philosophical interest and we may learn to modify it pharmacologically, and probably, on the record of technology for its own sake, to our hurt. But the study of the subject, if that study is, as I have suggested, by its own proper motion "religious," is bound to modify our social style and to qualify the limited intuitions of old-type objectivism, as Einsteinian insights qualified Newtonian without contradicting them. What occurs in a change of cultural style is that the universe of discourse is expanded, and every such expansion, in that it alters the "feel" of our experiences both of I and of That, is by the terms of our initial definition religious or "spiritual" in its content. It is this expansion, rather than a return to the numinous or the mysterious, that constitutes an augmented awareness of the sacral with which humanity finds itself in encounter.

References

1. Heisenberg, W., "The Representation of Nature in Contemporary Physics," *Daedalus* 87, 1958, pp. 95–108.
2. Mach, E. in J. R. Newman, *The World of Mathematics*, Simon & Schuster, New York, 1956, p. 1708.
3. Comfort, A., "Darwin and Freud," *Lancet* ii, 1960, pp. 107–11.
4. Freud, S., *The Ego and the Id*, Hogarth Press, London, 1927, p. 31.
5. Chāndogya Upaniṣad III, 13.
6. Chāndogya Upaniṣad III, 14.
7. Ornstein, R. E., *The Psychology of Consciousness*, Freeman, New York, 1972.
8. Bṛhad-āraṇyaka Upaniṣad III, 4, ii.
9. Barden, G., "Reflections of Time," *Human Context* 5, 1973, pp. 331–44.
10. Śrīmad Bhāgavatam I, 6, xviii.
11. Deikman, A. J., "Experimental Meditation," *Journal of Nervous and Mental Diseases* 136, 1963, pp. 329–43.
12. Bharati, A., *The Light at the Center*, Ross Erikson, Santa Barbara, 1976.
13. Hardy, A., *The Biology of God*, Jonathan Cape, London, 1975.
14. Mumford, Lewis, *The Myth of the Machine*, Harcourt, Brace, Jovanovitch, New York, 1970.
15. Medawar, P. B., *The Hope of Progress*, Methuen, London, 1972.
16. Feigl, H., *The Mental and the Physical*, U. Minn. Press, 1967.
17. Globus, G., "Unexplained symmetries in the 'world knot'," *Science* 180, pp. 1129–36.
18. Capra, F., *The Tao of Physics*, Lawrence Berkeley Laboratories Publications, California, LBL-796.
19. Davy, C., *Words in the Mind*, Chatto & Windus, London, 1965.
20. Westcott, J., "The Sculpture and Myths of the Eshu-Elegba, the Yoruba Trickster," *Africa* 32, 1962, pp. 336–54.
21. Comfort, A., "On Ecstasy and Originality," *Human Context* 1, 1969, pp. 243–58.
22. Koenig, O., in *The Nature of Human Behaviour*, ed. G. Altner, Allen & Unwin, 1976, ch. 5.
23. Wallace, A. F. C., *Religion: an anthropological view*, Random House, New York, 1966.
24. Whitehead, A. N., *Religion in the Making*, Cambridge University Press, 1926.
25. James, W., *The Varieties of Religious Experience*, Longman Green & Co., London, 1902.

26. Blake, W., *Marriage of Heaven and Hell*, p. 149.
27. Śaṅkara, *Commentary on the Kena Upaniṣad*, II, 4, Adyan Library, Madras, 1923.
28. Post, H., "Individuality and Physics," *Listener*, 10 November 1963.
29. Manilius, *Astronomica*, ed. A. E. Housman, Cambridge University Press, 1937.
30. Jung, C. G., *Psychology of the Unconscious*, Kegan Paul, Trench & Trubner, London, 1933.
31. Wasson, R. G., *Soma, the divine mushroom of immortality*, Harcourt, Brace, Jovanovich, New York, 1968.
32. Staal, F., *Exploring Mysticism*, Pelican, London, 1975.
33. Yinger, J. M., *The Scientific Study of Religion*, Macmillan, New York, 1970.
34. Speck, F. G., *Naskapi: The Savage Hunter of the Labrador Peninsula*, University of Oklahoma Press, 1953.
35. Wasson, R. G., Hofmann, A. and Ruck, C. A. P., *The Road to Eleusis*, Harcourt, Brace, Jovanovitch, New York and London, 1978.
36. Surajit Sinha in M. Singer, *Krishna: Myths, Rites and Attitudes*, University of Chicago Press, 1966.
37. Hivale, J., "The Dewar-bhaujī Relationship," *Man in India* 23, 1943, p. 159.
38. Skinner, B. F., *Beyond Freedom and Dignity*, Jonathan Cape, London, 1972.
39. Pribram, K., in Nicholas, J. M., *Images, Perception and Knowledge*, D. Reidel, Dordrecht, p. 155 seq., 1977.
40. Māhānirvāṇatantra 14, 115. Cited in Daniélou, A., see ref. 46.
41. Irenaeus i, 30.1.
42. Huxley, L. A., *The Timeless Moment*, Farrar, Straus & Giroux Inc., New York, 1968.
43. Zaehner, R. C., *Zen, Drugs and Mysticism*, Pantheon Press, New York, 1972.
44. Rawson, P., *The Art of Tantra*, Thames & Hudson, London, 1973.
45. Kullūka Bhatta, *Commentary on Manu Smṛti*, cited in Daniélou, A., see ref. 44.
46. Daniélou, A., *Hindu Polytheism*, Routledge & Kegan Paul, London, 1964.
47. Franck, A., *The Kabbalah, the Religious Philosophy of the Hebrews*, University Books, New York, 1967.
48. Argüelles, J. A., *The Transformative Vision*, Shambala Press, Berkeley, 1975.
49. Waters, F., *The Book of the Hopi*, Viking, New York, 1963.
50. *Church Family Newspaper*, 6 July 1923.

51. Waddington, C. H., *The Ethical Animal*, Allen & Unwin, London, 1960.
52. Haldane, J. B. S., *The Causes of Evolution*, Longman, London, 1932.
53. Hamilton, W. D., "Selfish and spiteful behaviour in an evolutionary model," *Nature* 228, 1970, pp. 1218–20.
54. Hardy, A., *The Biology of God*, Jonathan Cape, London, 1975.
55. Grof, S., Pahaka, W. N., Kurland, A. A. and Goodman, L. E., *LSD-assisted Psychotherapy in Patients with Terminal Cancer*, 5th Symposium of the Foundation of Thanatology, New York, 13 November 1971.
56. Yalom, I. D., *Existential Factors in Group Psychotherapy*, Strecker Memorial Lecture. *Strecker Monogr.* 11, Pennsylvania Hospital 1974.
57. Kālī Tantra. Cited by Daniélou, A. See ref. 46.
58. Comfort, A., "The position of ageing studies," *Mechanisms of Ageing and Development* 3, 1974, pp. 1–32.
59. Ader, R. and Cohen, N., *Psychosomatic Medecine* 37, 1976, pp. 333–40.
60. Stein, M., Schiavi, R., and Camerino, M., *Science* 191, 1976, pp. 435–40.
61. McKeown, T., "A historical appraisal of the medical task," in *Medical History and Medical Care*, ed. G. McLachlan & T. McKeown, Oxford University Press, 1971.
62. Lalonde, M., *A New Perspective on the Health of Canadians*, Information Canada, 1974.
63. Feinstein, A., *Clinical Judgement*, Williams & Wilkins, Baltimore, 1967.

INDEX